D1881018

A PRACTICAL HANDBOOK OF THE URIYA OR ODIYA LANGUAGE

A PRACTICAL HANDBOOK OF THE URIYA OR ODIYA LANGUAGE

BY

T.J. MALTBY

URIYA-DHIRI PANI POT HORO KATOI

GYAN

Published by

Gyan Publishing House
5, Ansari Road
Daryaganj, New Delhi-110002
Phone: 011-47034999, 9811692060
E-mail: books@gyanbooks.com

Distribution Network
gyanbooks.com
India, USA, Canada, UK, Australia, France

ISBN : 978-81-212-3025-4 (PB)
First Published, 1874

2nd Impression 2020

Printed at: Gyan Press, Delhi.

A
Practical Handbook of the
Uriya or Odiya Language
Author: T. J. Maltby

ERRATA.

For a *read* everywhere á.

For n or ṇ at the end of a word *read* everywhere ñ.

Page 3, line 3, *for* ଅମ୍ବ *read* ଅମ୍ବ ámbo, a mango.

,, 5, ,, 22, *for* " bracelet" *read* " necklace."

,, 9, ,, 1, *for* " thiá" *read* " ṭhia."

,, 9, ,, 5, *for* ଅୟସ *read* ଅୟାସ áyáso, hardship.

,, 10, ,, 5, *for* " sobdo" *read* " s'obdo," a noise.

,, 10, ,, 9, *for* " sroddhá" *read* " s'roddhá," reverence.

,, 10, ,, 10, *for* " bráhmono" *read* " bráhmoṇo," a Brahmin.

,, 10, ,, 21 to 24, *for* n *read* ṇ.

,, 11, ,, 4, *for* " t" *read* " ṭ."

11, ,, 14, *for* the first y *read* j.

11, ,, 14, *for* the second ଯ *read* ୟ.

,, 12, last line, *for* the first " so" *read* " s'o."

,, 14, line 10, *for* " form" *read* " from."

,, 17, ,, 5, *for* ମନୁଷ୍ଯ *read* ମନୁଷ୍ୟ, monushyo.

,, 17, ,, 7, after " Bholo gotshománe" *read* good trees.

,, 17, ,, 13, *for* " bálika" *read* " báḷika," a girl.

,, 19, ,, 1, *for* ଅମ୍ଭେ *read* ଅମ୍ଭେ, ámbhe.

,, 30, ,, 7, *for* " tundo" *read* " tuṇḍo."

,, 31, ,, 7, *for* " káhiṇki" *read* " háhiñki."

,, 33, ,, 2, *for* " próti" *read* " proti."

,, 33, ,, 4, *for* " pokhi" *read* " pokhí."

,, 35, ,, 8, *for* କାଳି *read* କାଲି, káli.

,, 39, last line but one, after ଉଚ୍ଛି *read* କର.

,, 43, line 9, *for* " disuchhi" *read* " dis'uchhi."

,, 45, ,, 11, *for* ସାଖୀକ *read* ସାଖୀକି, ṣákhíki.

Page 47, line 10, *for* " soye" *read* " s'oye."

" 50, " 3, *for* " káḷi" *read* " k ili."

" 51, " 8, *for* ଲେଖିବାର *read* ଲେଖିବାରେ, lekhibáre.

" 53, " 3, *for* ବେଲକୁ *read* ବେଳକୁ, beḷoku.

" 53, last line, *for* " s'áloku" *read* " s'áḷoku."

" 56, line 2, *for* ଗୁଲି *read* ଗୁଳି, guḷi, bullet.

" 57, last line, *for* " poko" *read* " póko" insect.

" 58, line 1, *for* " hoṅgso" *read* " hongso."

" 61, " 8, *for* ଟାକୁ *read* ଟାଙ୍କୁ, tángku.

" 63, " 4, *for* " tant" *read* " taut."

" 68, " 8, *for* " tshoṇre" *read* " ts-hoṇore."

" 68, " 10, *for* ଲଗବ *read* ଲଗିବ.

" 73 and 79, *for* BA'NGMU'LO *read* BA'NGMU'ḶO.

" 75, line 5, insert " huri" before " koli."

" 89, " 2, *for* " Tonkhilá" *read* " Tonikhilá."

" 93, " 19, *for* " gáli" *read* " gáḷi," abuse.

" 95, " 9, *for* " gótie" *read* " góṭie."

" 95, " 16, *for* " rosuniá" *read* " rosuṇiá."

" 111, last line but one, *for* " moro" *read* " móro."

" 119, line 8, *for* " Bodogoḍo" *read* " Boḍogoḍo."

" 125, " 6, *for* " jogyoko" *read* " jógkyoko."

" 125, *for* ୨ *read* ୭ Soptomo, &c.

" 131, " 20, *for* " jobábo" *read* " dzobábo."

" 133, " 9, *for* ୧ *read* ୧୫ pondoro.

" 135, " 5, *for* " ko-pori" *read* " kópori."

" 143, " 23, *for* " rondzángku" *read* " rodzángku."

" 145, " 16, *for* " guli" *read* " guḷi."

PREFACE.

THE chief object which I have had in compiling this Handbook is to supply an existing want in a practical shape, as with the exception of Dr. Sutton's Introduction to Uriya, which was published about a generation ago, there is no book I know of, that will assist the Englishman in learning the Uriya language.

The plan adopted will, it is hoped, smooth over many difficulties, and make the language easy of acquisition by any one desiring to obtain a colloquial and useful knowledge of it.

Uriya, or rather O'ḍiyá, is chiefly spoken in the Districts of Orissa in Bengal, and Ganjam in Madras, but the language is by no means confined to them, and extends over a much wider area of country than is usually supposed. Owing, however, to the countries in which Uriya is spoken being under the rule of three separate Governments, *viz.*, Bengal, Madras, and the Central Provinces, the limits of the language have never been exactly ascertained. Its spoken area is irregular in shape, and extends in one line along the sea-coast from Midnapore in Bengal to Barwah, a small seaport town in Ganjam, a distance of 350 miles. From this point the language strikes inwards, leaving the sea-board free to Telugu, and continues to withdraw deeper and deeper inland, the farther it runs south, until it reaches its extreme limit amongst the Maliahs of Jeypore in the District of Vizagapatam. The language then runs northwards as far as Raigarh in the Central Provinces, and may be said to cease about half way between Sumbulpore and Raipore. It will thus be seen that the Uriya-speaking tract of country resembles a quadrilateral figure of four unequal sides, and contains an approximate area of 60,000 square miles. Amidst the mountainous tracts however of the ancient kingdom of Orissa dwell the wild tribes of Kols, Gonds, Kondhs, and Souras who each speak a language of their own. Their numbers must therefore be deducted in estimating the Uriya population. I append the names of the different Districts in which Uriya is spoken together with their approximate population.

Bengal Presidency.

District of Midnapore,	2,000,000
——— Balasore,	770,232
——— Cuttack,	1,494,784
——— Puri,	769,674
The 29 Tributary States of Orissa,	1,283,309

Central Provinces.

District of Sumbulpore, ...	1,152,534

Madras.

District of Ganjam, ...	1,000,000
(Two-thirds of the total population reckoned as Uriyas.)	

Jeypore in Vizagapatam.

Jeypore, in Vizagapatam, ...	429,513
Total,	8,900,040

Deducting one million as the probable population of the wild Hill tribes, we obtain a total Uriya population of close upon *eight millions*, without reckoning the Uriyas of Calcutta and Chota Nagpore.

The wildness and inaccessibility of the greater part of the country in which the Uriyas live will doubtless account for the backwardness of its inhabitants; and the small share of attention which their language has hitherto attracted, is rather due to this fact, than to the want of any intrinsic merits of its own.

Uriya is bounded north of Midnapore by Bengali, on the South by Telugu, and on the West by Hindustani. Its distinctive peculiarity is the frequent occurrence of the "o" sound, which gives it an accidental resemblance to Italian or Spanish, although I am not prepared to state that this resemblance goes much further. The practice of representing the first letter of the Uriya alphabet by the English letter "a" is, however, calculated to convey an erroneous impression of this peculiarity. The vowel ଅ should therefore be invariably rendered by the letter "o" pronounced short. Dr. Sutton himself admits this when he says that the sound of the Uriya letter ଅ is that of "a" in the word "what," but the same sound would in this instance be more correctly rendered by the same word if spelt "wot." Uriya is not a difficult language to learn, but its character is probably the most awkward of Oriental ones, although its alphabet is a very complete one and resembles the Sanskrit. The language is an ancient one, and its literature by no means inconsiderable. Most of its works, however, seem to be identical with the corresponding ones in Sanskrit, and cannot therefore lay claim to much originality. The purest Uriya is spoken in Gumsur, and north of the Rushikuliá river, as owing to Bengali being the official language in Orissa, and its having a considerable affinity to Uriya, the latter seems to have assimilated to it more than to Telugu in the south. The most esteemed author amongst the Uriyas, Upendro Bhondzo, was a Rajah of Gumsur, and although local differences of speech and writing exist, it may be taken for granted that pure Uriya is generally understood throughout the whole of the ancient kingdom of Orissa. Uriya is also the language into which Kondh and Soura are translated, when evidence in either of those languages is given in the public Courts.

This book consists of five parts :—

1*stly.*—An Explanation of the Uriya alphabet and the more necessary elements of grammar.

2*ndly.*—*Practical sentences* in the Roman and Uriya character obtained from natives. If any body wants to learn Uriya, and will master these sentences thoroughly, he will find himself the possessor of a fair knowledge of the language.

3*rdly.*—Extracts in the Roman character from cases mostly taken down from the lips of the speakers themselves, so as to illustrate the genius of the spoken language, and as an assistance towards acquiring the native style of conversation, instead of a European one.

4*thly.*—Specimens with translations of the ordinary style of business letters on various topics.

5*thly.*—The "Níti Kothá," a small collection of Fables used as a reading-book in schools, and also some useful official terms and the Uriya numerals. An attempt has thus been made to illustrate the three different phases (leaving the poetical one out of the question) *viz.* the *colloquial*, the *epistolary*, and the *prose style* of the language, in what I conceive to be the consecutive order of their importance in acquiring a useful practical knowledge of Uriya. I have abstained from attempting to give any undue prominence to the grammatical portion, as a mere knowledge of Grammar, however perfect, can no more teach a man to *speak* a language, than a knowledge of the science of music will teach him to play on the fiddle.

Practice in conversation, combined with a parrot-like imitation of the native pronunciation, is the only way to acquire a useful knowledge of any language. Never let the learner lose an opportunity of bringing what he knows into practice, no matter how small that knowledge may be, and with this object in view he must *lay aside all hesitation in speaking*. As a hint I would strongly recommend him always to *read the language aloud*, whether by himself or with a munshi, in order that he may accustom his ear to the sounds and acquire a correct pronunciation. Most people who attempt to learn a strange tongue begin by learning to read and write it. This is, however, a great mistake if their object is to learn to *speak*, as the more natural course is first to acquire a colloquial knowledge and afterwards to learn to read and write. For further remarks upon this subject, however, I would refer the learner to the " Mastery of Languages" by T. Prendergast, Esq., late Madras Civil Service, which is by far the best book upon the subject I have ever read.

With regard to the employment of the Roman character, I must observe that there are at present no means of acquiring an entrance into Uriya without being first obliged to wade through the mysteries, intricacies and uninviting difficulty of the Uriya alphabet. The crabbed hieroglyphics of native languages justify in my opinion any attempt to escape from their thralls, and when it is considered that this great stumbling-block in the shape of native alphabets is sufficient to prevent the greater number of our countrymen and countrywomen in India from ever attempting to learn the native languages, the great usefulness of the Roman alphabet in assisting to overcome this difficulty cannot fail to be recognized by all who consider the subject in an intelligent spirit. In romanising the Uriya character, I have taken all the care I could to ensure a correct pronunciation, and I trust that the arrangement of the alphabet and the explanations given therein will be sufficient to remove any doubts that may be entertained by the learner. One of the greatest advantages of beginning an Oriental language in the Roman character is, that *it enables the learner to make use of the language at once*, and thus encourages him to persevere. As Professor Wilson has however stated that the only trustworthy representation of an Indian word is its native costume, and that it can never be thoroughly nationalised in any other,

I do not advocate the employment of the Roman character with the object of supplanting the native one, but in order to render the acquisition of the latter more easy to all who desire to gain a fair knowledge of the language. I believe, however, that it is quite as possible to acquire a good pronunciation of Uriya with the use of the Roman character, as with its own, provided that the English pronunciation of the Roman letters be discarded, and the German or Italian substituted, and I can advise all European magistrates and others who are required to take down statements in the vernacular, *to do so in the Roman character.* A comparatively slight acquaintance with a language, and a good ear will enable a man to do this correctly, and he will find the practise an excellent one if he wishes to obtain a mastery of the language, besides being more likely to ensure the accuracy of the statements made before him. It is hoped that this book, although professedly for Europeans learning Uriya, may also be found useful to Uriyas learning English. And although the writer is aware that it is susceptible of improvement, yet he trusts that the mistakes are not such as to mar its usefulness.

In conclusion I take this opportunity of calling the attention of Government to the necessity that seems to exist for *the compilation of a more or less uniform series of Handbooks*, adapted to each of the different languages spoken in India. Competent persons might be selected to compile such a Handbook for every part of the country in which a distinct language prevails, and the Series might agree in its main particulars, so as to go hand in hand with the present collection of District Manuals now in course of preparation. In carrying out this scheme, the object to be attained, viz., a practical colloquial knowledge of each language should be chiefly aimed at, and I think that if this were done, and useless matter excluded, every one would recognize the utility of such a compilation. In many instances the want of such Handbooks to assist in bringing the governors and the governed more into contact, as in the case of so many of the numerous Hill tribes that exist in India, must force itself upon the conviction of all who give the matter their consideration.

The great importance to the administration of a knowledge on the part of public officers of the languages spoken by the people with whom they have to deal, seems to have been, to use their own words, lately prominently brought to the notice of the Government of India, and they have recently called for a general report as to the knowledge possessed by District officers of the less known, and more remote languages (Uriya amongst the number), in consequence of their having reason to fear that such languages were by no means generally known by officers living amongst the people they governed.

As regards many of the Hill languages, no means of acquiring them from books exists, and the necessity of Government promoting the compilation of Handbooks in such instances is sufficiently obvious, if they wish their officers to possess any real influence with the people, and the material welfare of the country to be developed.

In cases where no written character exists, as in Kondh, it is of the highest importance that the Roman character only should be used and adapted to the language. It is likely that such a course would ultimately have a most civilizing effect upon the wild Hill Tribes by narrowing the gulf that exists between them and the learning of the West.

The issue of the proposed Series might therefore begin with the less known languages and be gradually extended to those better known, for the compilation of which ample materials already exist. With regard to the latter, the only thing which would remain to be done, would be to give the material employed a definite method, and some plan of recognized usefulness, and these details might easily be settled by a properly qualified Committee appointed by Government.

As, however, the mere enunciation of such an idea without a practical illustration of what is in my humble opinion most required in acquiriug a useful knowledge of a language, would not be of much avail, I beg to submit this book to the public as my part of the contribution towards carrying out the scheme, which I have ventured to suggest.

Berhampore, October, 1873.

URIYA ALPHABET.

The URIYA alphabet contains 50 letters. For easy reference the order of the ENGLISH alphabet has been observed.

DENTAL letters should be pronounced by applying the tongue to the teeth.

CEREBRAL letters can only be properly pronounced by turning the tip of the tongue upwards against the roof of the mouth.

URIYA words in the ROMAN character are to be pronounced as in GERMAN or ITALIAN rather than as in ENGLISH, and care must be taken that every letter be distinctly sounded.

It must be noted that the vowel ଅ pronounced like "o" in "not," is inherent in every consonant.

Uriya Letters.

Roman Letters.		Initial.		Medial.
A	a	ଅ	has the sound of short "o," and is invariably written so, ...	—
A′	á	ଆ	is pronounced like á in father, ...	ା
B	b	ବ	pronounced singly as "b," in combination as "w,"	—
Bh	bh	ଭ	the aspirate of b pronounced by breathing hardly upon it, ...	—
Ch	ch	ଚ	softly pronounced like "ts" when not combined with e, i, or í, ...	—
Chh	chh	ଛ	the above letter aspirated, ...	—
D	d	ଦ	the dental or soft "d" as in "did,"	—
Dh	dh	ଧ	the above letter aspirated, ...	—
Ḍ	ḍ	ଡ	the cerebral or hard ḍ as in the word "ḍoll,"	—
Ḍh	ḍh	ଢ	the aspirate of the above letter,......	—
E	e	ଏ	pronounced both long as in "ale" and short as in "end,"	
G	g	ଗ	pronounced like the "g" in "gaudy,"	—
Gh	gh	ଘ	the above letter aspirated, ...	—
H	h	ହ	the Uriya aspirate, ...	—

Examples.

ଅନେକ onéko, many. ବଳଦ boḷodo, a bullock.

ଆଖୁ ákhu, sugarcane. ଆଖି ákhi, the ėye. ପାଣି páṇi, water.

ବାଟ báṭo, a road. ଆମ୍ବ ámbo, a mango. ଜ୍ୱର dzworo fever.

ଭାତ bháto, boiled rice. ଭୋଜନ bhódzono, eating. ଭଲ bholo, good.

ଚିଠାଉ chiṭáu, a letter. ଚାଲ tsálo, go on. ଚାଉଳ tsáuḷo, rice.

ଛତା ts-hotá, an umbrella. ଛୋଟା ts-hóṭá, lame. ଛିଡ଼ା chhiḍá, standing.

ଦାନ dáno, a gift. ଦେଉଳ deuḷo, a temple. ଦେବାର debáro, to give.

ଧାନ dháno, corn. ଧରିବାର dhoribáro, to seize. ଧନୁ dhonu, a bow.

ଡାଳ ḍáḷo, a branch. ଡରିବାର ḍoribáro, to fear. ହାଣ୍ଡି háṇḍi, an earthen pot.

ଢାଳ ḍháḷo, a brass pot. ଢାଲ ḍhálo, a shield.

ଏଗାର egáro, eleven. କେସେ kese, who? କେତେ kete, how many?

ଗଡ godo, a fort. ଗୋଡ଼ góḍo, the leg. ଗାତ gáto, a hole.

ଘେରିବାର gheribáro, to surround. ଘର ghoro, a house. ଘରା ghorá, a nest.

ହାତ háto, the hand. ହାଟ háṭo, a market. ହାଣିବାର háṇibáro, to cut.

Uriya Letters.

Roman Letters.	Initial.			Medial.
H	h	ଃ	the Sanskrit "visarga,"...............	—
I	i	ଇ	pronounced short as in "bit,"	
I′	í	ଈ	pronounced long as in "políce,"...	ୀ
J	j	ଜ	has more frequently the true sound of "j" than the next letter, ...	—
J	j	ଯ	is nearly always pronounced "dz," but combined with "i" or "í," like "j,"...........................	—
Jh	jh	ଝ	the above letter aspirated, ...	—
K	k	କ	pronounced as in the word "kill,"...	—
Kh	kh	ଖ	the above letter aspirated, ...	—
Ksh	ksh	କ୍ଷ	is pronounced like "kḥy,"...........	—
L	l	ଲ	the soft l as in "love,"	—
Ḷ	ḷ	ଳ	the cerebral ḷ as in "ḷoud,"	[illegible]
M	m	ମ	corresponds to the English "m," ...	[illegible]
N	n	ନ	the soft "n" as in "never,"	——

Example.

ଦୁଃଖ duhkho, sorrow.

ଇଟ୍ଟା iṭṭá, a brick. ବିଲମ୍ବ biḷombo, delay. ବିକିବାର biki-báro, to sell.

ଈଶ୍ୱର ís'woro, God. ଧୀରେ dhíre, slowly. ନୀଳୀ níḷí indigo.

ଯୁଦ୍ଧ juddho, war. ଯେବେ jebe, if, when. ଯିବାର jibáro, to go.

ଜାଲ dzálo, a net. ଜାଳିବାର dzáḷibáro, to burn. ଜିଣିବାର jiṇibáro, to conquer.

ଝାଳ dzháḷo, perspiration. ଝିଅ jhio, a daughter. ଝିଂକିବାର jhinkibáro, to pull.

କରିବାର koribáro, to do. ଶୁଷ୍କ s'ushko, dry. କନ୍ଧ kondho, a KONDH.

ଖନ୍ଦ khondo, a crop. ଖଣ୍ଡ khoṇḍo, a piece. ଖୋଳିବାର khóḷibáro, to dig.

କ୍ଷମା khyomá, pardon. କ୍ଷୁଦ୍ର khyudro, mean, petty. ଅକ୍ଷର okhyoṛo, a letter.

ଲତା lotá, bramble, scrub jungle. ଲୋଟା lóṭá, a brass vessel. ବିଲ bilo, a paddy-field.

ବିଳା biḷá, an ant-hill. ମଳିବାର moḷibáro, to tread out corn. ଶୁକ୍ଳ s'ukḷo, white.

ମାଲ málo, property. ମାଳ máḷo, bracelet. ଜନ୍ମ dzonmo, birth.

ନଦୀ nodí, a river. ଭିନ୍ନ bhinno, different. ମନ୍ଦ mondo, bad.

Uriya Letters.

Roman Letters.		Initial.		Medial.
Ṇ	ṇ	ଣ	the cerebral ṇ pronounced nearly as in "ṇaughty,"	—
Ng	ng	ଙ	nasal letter pronounced as in 'sung,'	—
O′	ó	ଓ	usually pronounced long, ...	ୋ
Oi	oi	ଐ	pronounced as in "hoist,"	ୈ
Ou	ou	ଔ	pronounced as in the word "out,"...	ୌ
P	p	ପ	corresponds to the English p, ...	—
Ph	ph	ଫ	the above letter aspirated as in "up-hill,"	—
R	r	ର	corresponds to the English r, ...	୍ର ର୍
Ru	ru	ଋ	pronounced as in "quádruple,"......	ୃ
Rú	rú	ୠ	pronounced as in "rúle,"	ୄ
S	s	ସ	pronounced as in "sorrow,"	—
S′	s′	ଶ	pronounced nearly like the "sh" in "shall,"	—
Sh	sh	ଷ	pronounced as in "shut,"............	—
T	t	ତ	the dental or soft "t," as in "till,"	—
Th	th	ଥ	the aspirate of the above, ...	
Ṭ	ṭ	ଟ	the cerebral ṭ pronounced hard as in "ṭall,"........................	—

Examples.

କଣ koṇo, what? ପଣସ poṇoso, the jack fruit. ବିଷ୍ଣୁ Bishṇu, Vishnu.

ବାଙ୍ମୂଳ bángmúḷo, deposition. ବାଂଶ báṅgs'o bamboo. ଲୋକଙ୍କୁ lókongku, to the people.

ଓଡ଼ିଆ óḍiyá, Uriya. ଓଟ óṭo, a camel. ଓଠ óṭho, the lip. ଘୋଡ଼ା ghóḍá, a horse.

ଐକ୍ୟ oikyo, unity. ବୈଦ୍ୟ boidyo, a physician.

ଔଷଧ oushodho, medicine. ଦୌଡ଼ି douḍi, running.

ପତ୍ର potro, a leaf, ପଥର pothoro, a stone. ପଠାଇବାର poṭháibáro, to send.

ଫୁଲ phulo, a flower. ଫଳ phoḷo, fruit. ଫୁଲିବାର phulibáro, to swell.

ରଖିବାର rokhibáro, to place. ବଜ୍ର bodzro, a thunderbolt. ମୂର୍ଖ múrkho, foolish.

ଋଣ ruṇo, debt. ମୃଗ mrugo, a stag.

ରୂପ rúpo, shape, form.

ସତ soto, true. ସହଜ sohodzo, easy. ସରପରା soroporá, a supply.

ଶବ s'obo, a corpse. ଶୁଆ s'uá, a parrot. ଦର୍ଶନ dors'ono, a visit.

ଷଣ୍ଢ shoṇḍo, a bull. ପୋଷିଆ póshiá, adopted.

ଚଷା tosá, a cultivator. ତାଳ táḷo, the palmyra. ଯତ୍ନ jotno, an effort. ରକ୍ତ rokto, blood.

ଥଣ୍ଟ thoṇṭo, the beak. ଥାଳ tháḷo, a plate. ଥରେ thore, once.

ଟଙ୍କା ṭonká, a rupee. ଫୁଟିବାର phuṭibáro, to burst. ଟାଙ୍ଗୀ ṭángí, an axe, an halbert.

URIYA LETTERS.

Roman Letters.	Initial.			Medial
Ṭh	ṭh	ଠ	the above cerebral aspirated, ...	—
U	u	ଉ	pronounced as in the word, "truth,"	ୁ
Ū	u	ଊ	pronounced long as in "prúne," ..	ୂ
Y	y	ୟ	pronounced as in "yes,"	୍ୟ

The consonant ଞ "nyo" occurs only in combination, and has therefore been omitted from the above scheme, but occurs further on.

The 2 vowels ଌ lu and ୡ lú have also been omitted, as they are but seldom used.

Examples.

ଠିଆ thiá, standing. ଉଠିବାର uṭhibáro, to lift, raise.
ଉଇ ui, a white-ant. ଉପର uporo, above, the upper part. କୁକ୍କୁର kukkuro, a dog.
ଊରୁ úru, a thigh. କୁଅଁ kuoṇ, a well.
ଆୟସ áyaso, hardship. ବାକ୍ୟ bákyo, a sentence.

Combinations.

The following scheme comprises the principal changes that occur in the combination of two or more Uriya letters.

Roman.	Uriya.	Examples.
B and d	ବ and ଦ form ବ୍ଦ	ଶବ୍ଦ sobdo, a noise.
Ch and ch	ଚ and ଚ form ଚ୍ଚ	ଉଚ୍ଚ uts-tso, high.
Ch and chh	ଚ and ଛ form ଚ୍ଛ	ଅଚ୍ଛା áts-tshá, good.
D and bh	ଦ and ଭ form ଦ୍ଭ	ଅଦ୍ଭୁତ odbhuto, wonderful
D and dh	ଦ and ଧ form ଦ୍ଧ	ଶ୍ରଦ୍ଧା sroddhá, reverence.
H and m	ହ and ମ form ହ୍ମ	ବ୍ରାହ୍ମଣ bráhmono, a Brahmin.
J and ny	ଜ and ଞ form ଜ୍ଞ	ଜ୍ଞାନ gyáno, wisdom. ବିଜ୍ଞ bigyon, wise.
K and r	କ and ର form କ୍ର	କ୍ରମେକ୍ରମେ kromekrome, by degrees.
M and bh	ମ and ଭ form ମ୍ଭ	ଆମ୍ଭେ ámbhe, I, we.
M and p	ମ and ପ form ମ୍ପ	ସମ୍ପତ୍ତି sompotti, possession.
N and d	ନ and ଦ form ନ୍ଦ	ସୁନ୍ଦର sundoro, beautiful.
N and dh	ନ and ଧ form ନ୍ଧ	ଅନ୍ଧାର ondháro, dark.
N and t	ନ and ତ form ନ୍ତ	ଦାନ୍ତ dánto, a tooth.
N and th	ନ and ଥ form ନ୍ଥ	କାନ୍ଥ kántho, a wall.
N and ḍ	ଣ and ଡ form ଣ୍ଡ	ଦାଣ୍ଡ dánḍo, road.
N and ḍh	ଣ and ଢ form ଣ୍ଢ	ମେଣ୍ଢା menḍhá, a sheep.
N and ṭ	ଣ and ଟ form ଣ୍ଟ	କଣ୍ଟା konṭá, a thorn.
N and ṭh	ଣ and ଠ form ଣ୍ଠ	କଣ୍ଠ konṭho, the throat.
Ng and k	ଙ and କ form ଙ୍କ	ବାଙ୍କ bánko, crooked.
Ny and ch	ଞ and ଚ form ଞ୍ଚ	ଲାଞ୍ଚ lántso, a bribe.

Ny and chh ଞ and ଛ form ଞ୍ଛ ଲାଞ୍ଛନା lánts-honá, a rebuke.

Ny and dz ଞ and ଜ form ଞ୍ଜ ଲାଞ୍ଜ lándzo, a tail.

S and t ସ and ତ form ସ୍ତ ସ୍ତନ stháno, a place.

Sh and t ଷ and ଟ form ଷ୍ଟ କଷ୍ଟ koshṭo, trouble.

T and r ତ and ର form ତ୍ର ପୁତ୍ରା putrá, a nephew.

T and t ତ and ତ form ତ୍ତ ଉତ୍ତମ uttomo, excellent.

T and th ତ and ଥ form ତ୍ଥ ଉତ୍ଥାନ uttháno, steep.

Combinations of three letters.

R t and th, ରତ and ଥ, form ର୍ଥ. Example, ପ୍ରାର୍ଥନା prárthoná, a prayer.

R d and dh, ରଦ and ଧ, form ର୍ଦ୍ଧ. Example, ବର୍ଦ୍ଧନ borddhono, an increase.

R y and v, ରଯ and ଯ, form ର୍ଯ୍ୟ. Example, କାର୍ଯ୍ୟ kárjyo, an affair.

S t and u, ସତ and ଉ, form ସ୍ତୁ. Example, ବସ୍ତୁ bostu, a thing.

Vowels.

ଅ ଆ ଇ ଈ ଉ ଊ

ଋ ୠ ଌ ୡ ଏ ଐ

ଓ ଔ ଅଂ ଅଃ

Consonants.

କ ଖ ଗ ଘ ଙ

ଚ ଛ ଜ ଝ ଞ

ଟ ଠ ଡ ଢ ଣ

ତ ଥ ଦ ଧ ନ

ପ ଫ ବ ଭ ମ

ଯ ର ଲ ବ ଶ

ଷ ସ ହ କ୍ଷ ।

Uriya consonants are 34 in number, and are classified as follows :—

1. Gutturals, କ ko ଖ kho ଗ go ଘ gho ଙ gno.
2. Palatals, ଚ tso ଛ tsho ଜ dzo ଝ dzho ଞ nyọ.
3. Cerebrals, ଟ ṭo ଠ ṭho ଡ ḍo ଢ ḍho ଣ oro.
4. Dentals, ତ to ଥ tho ଦ do ଧ dho ନ no.
5. Labials, ପ po ଫ pho ବ bo ଭ bho ମ mo.
6. Miscellaneous, ଯ jo ର ro ଳ ḷo ଲ lo ବ vo ଶ so ଷ sho ସ so ହ ho, କ୍ଷ khyo.

GRAMMAR.

The following elements of Uriya Grammar contain, it is hoped, all that it is most essential for a learner to know.

Nouns.

Nouns in Uriya are declined as below :—

Singular.

Nominative	ଘର ghoro, a house.
Genitive	ଘରର ghororo, of a house.
Dative	ଘରକୁ ghoroku, to a house.
Accusative	ଘରକୁ ghoroku, a house.
Locative	{ ଘରେ ghore, or / ଘରରେ ghorore } in a house.
	ଘରଠାରେ ghoroṭháre, at a house
Ablative	{ ଘରରୁ ghororu / ଘରଠାରୁ ghoroṭháru } from a house.

The plural number is formed by adding to the singular the termination ମାନେ máne, which is sometimes abbreviated into ଏ e, as ଲୋକ lóko, a person; plural ଲୋକମାନେ lókománe, or ଲୋକେ lóke, persons.

Plural.

NOMINATIVE	ଘରମାନେ ghorománe, houses.
GENITIVE	ଘରମାନଙ୍କର ghorománongkoro. of houses.
DATIVE	ଘରମାନଙ୍କୁ ghorománongku, to houses.
ACCUSATIVE	ଘରମାନଙ୍କୁ ghorománongku, houses.
LOCATIVE	ଘରମାନଙ୍କରେ ghorománongkore, in houses. ଘରମାନଙ୍କଠାରେ ghorománongkoṭháre, at houses.
INSTRUMENTAL	ଘରମାନଙ୍କରେ ghorománongkore, by houses.
ABLATIVE	{ ଘରମାନଙ୍କରୁ ghorománongkoru, ଘରମାନଙ୍କଠାରୁ ghorománongkoṭháru. } form houses.

ABBREVIATIONS of the plural are not uncommon, as ଲୋକଙ୍କର lókongkoro, of the people, instead of ଲୋକମାନଙ୍କର lókománongkoro, &c., &c.

PRONOUNS.

The personal pronouns are four: ମୁଁ mun, I; ତୁ tu, thou; ସେ se, he; and ତାହା táhá, it.

The honorific forms are ଆମ୍ଭେ ámbhe, I, ତୁମ୍ଭେ tumbhe, you, and ଆପଣ ápono, which may be rendered by "your honour," and requires the verb to be in the plural number.

The pronouns ମୁଁ mun I, ତୁ tu, thou, and ସେ se, he, are thus declined:

ମୁ mu, I.

Singular.

Nominative	ମୁଁ mun, I.
Genitive	ମୋର móro, mine.
Dative / Accusative	ମୋତେ móte, to me, or me.

Plural.

Nominative	ଆମ୍ଭେମାନେ ámbhemáne, we.
Genitive	ଆମ୍ଭମାନଙ୍କର ámbhománongkoro, ours.
Dative / Accusative	ଅମ୍ଭମାନଙ୍କୁ ámbhománongku, to us.

ତୁ tu, thou.

Singular.

Nominative	ତୁ tu, thou.
Genitive	ତୋର tóro, thine.
Dative / Accusative	ତୋତେ tóte, to thee, or thee.

Plural.

Nominative	ତୁମ୍ଭେମାନେ tumbhemáne, you.
Genitive	ତୁମ୍ଭମାନଙ୍କର tumbhománongkoro, yours.
Dative / Accusative	ତୁମ୍ଭମାନଙ୍କୁ tumbhománongku, to you, or you.

ସେ se, he.

Singular.

Nominative	ସେ se, he.
Genitive	ତାର táro, his.
Dative / Accusative	ତାକୁ táku, to him or him.

Plural.

NOMINATIVE ସେମାନେ semáne, they.
GENITIVE ତାହାଙ୍କର táhángkoro, or ତାଙ୍କର tángkoro, theirs.
DATIVE / ACCUSATIVE } ତାହାଙ୍କୁ táhángku or ତାଙ୍କୁ tángkụ, to them, or them.

In the plural ସେମାନଙ୍କର semánongkoro, theirs, and ସେମାନଙ୍କୁ, semánongku to them, are also used.

The relative pronoun ଯେଉଁ jeuṇ, who or which, is declined as follows :—

Singular.

NOMINATIVE ଯେଉଁ jeuṇ, who, which.
GENITIVE ଯାହାର jáháro, of whom.
DATIVE / ACCUSATIVE } ଯାହାକୁ jáháku, to whom.

Plural.

NOMINATIVE ଯେଉଁମାନେ jeuṇmáne.
GENITIVE ଯାହାଙ୍କର jáhángkoro.
DATIVE / ACCUSATIVE } ଯାହାଙ୍କୁ jáhangku.

The interrogative pronouns are କି ki, କିସ kiso, କଣ kono, what? for things, and କେସେ kese, କେ ke, and କୋ kó, who? for persons. କେସେ kese, who? is thus declined :

Singular.

NOMINATIVE କେସେ kese, who?
GENITIVE କାହାର káháro, and କାର karo whose?
DATIVE କାହାକୁ káháku, to whom.

Plural.

NOMINATIVE	କୋମାନେ komane.
GENITIVE	କୋମାନଙ୍କର kómánongkoro.
DATIVE	କୋମାନଙ୍କୁ kómanongku.

ADJECTIVES.

URIYA adjectives remain, as a rule, unaffected by either gender, number, or case: as, ଭଲ ମନୁଷ୍ୟ Bholo monushyo, a good man, ଭଲ ମାଇକିନିଆ Bholo maikiniá, a good woman, ଭଲ ଗଛମାନେ Bholo gots-homane.

THE affixes of URIYA adjectives are most of them derived from the SANSKRIT, and in a few instances it is the custom to retain their distinctive form in the feminine gender, as ସେ ଏକ ବୁଢ଼ି ମାଇକିନିଆ Sé eko buḍhi máikiniá, she is an old woman, ସେ ବାଳିକା ସୁନ୍ଦରୀ Se báliká sunḍori, that is a pretty girl.

COMPARISON is expressed either by means of the ablative case, or by means of the word ପ୍ରତି proti, the second object compared being placed first in the sentence; as,

ଛେଳିଠାରୁ ଗାଇ ଭଲ. Chheḷiṭháru gai bholo. Lit. than a goat a cow good; a cow is better than a goat, or, ଛେଳିକି ପ୍ରତି ଗାଇ ଭଲ Chheḷiki proti gái bholo.

THE superlative is usually expressed with the assistance of the word ସବୁ sobu, all, or ସମସ୍ତ somosto, all, joined to the object compared; as,

ସବୁ ମନୁଷ୍ୟଠାରୁ ସେ ଭଲ Sobu monushyoṭharu se bholo, he is the best of men.

THE word ମଧ୍ୟରେ modhyore, in the midst of, is also employed to express the superlative ; as,

ସବୁ ମନୁଷ୍ୟ ମଧ୍ୟରେ ସେ ଭଲ Sobu monushyo modhyore se bholo, he is the best of men.

VERBS.

THE principal auxiliary verbs are ଥିବାର Thibáro, to be or to remain.

And ହୋଇବାର Hóibáro, or ହେବାର Hebáro, to be or to become.

ଥିବାର Thibáro, to be, is thus conjugated :

PRESENT TENSE.

Person	Singular.
1st	ମୁ ଅଛି mu ochhi, I am.
2nd	ତୁ ଅଛୁ tu ots-hu, thou art.
3rd	ସେ ଅଛି sė ochhi, he is.
	Plural.
1st	ଆମ୍ଭେ ଅଛୁ ámbhe ots-hu, we are.
2nd	ତୁମ୍ଭେ ଅଛ tumbhe ots-ho, you are.
3rd	ସେମାନେ ଅଛନ୍ତି semáne ots-honti, they are.

PAST TENSE.

I was.

Person	Singular.
1st	ମୁ ଥିଲି mu thili, I was.
2nd	ତୁ ଥିଲୁ tu thilu, thou wert.
3rd	ସେ ଥିଲା se thilá, he was.

Person Plural.

1st ଅମ୍ଭେ ଥିଲୁ ámbhe thilu, we were.

2nd ତୁମ୍ଭେ ଥିଲ tumbhe thilo, you were.

3rd ସେମାନେ ଥିଲେ semáne thile, they were.

Future Tense.

I will be.

Person Singular.

1st ମୁ ଥିବି mu thibi, I will be.

2nd ତୁ ଥିବୁ tu thibu, thou wilt be.

3rd ସ ଥିବ se thibo, he will be.

Plural.

1st ଅମ୍ଭେ ଥିବୁ ámbhe thibu, we will be.

2nd ତୁମ୍ଭେ ଥିବ tumbhe thibo, you will be.

3rd ସେ ମାନେ ଥିବେ semáne thibe, they will be.

Imperative Mood.

Be.

Person Singular.

1st ମୁ ଥାଏ mu tháe, let me be.

2nd ତୁ ଥା tu thá, be.

3rd ସେ ଥାଉ se tháu, let him be.

Plural.

1st ଅମ୍ଭେ ଥାଉ ámbhe tháu, let us be.

2nd ତୁମ୍ଭେ ଥାଅ tumbhe tháo, be ye.

3rd ସେମାନେ ଥାନ୍ତୁ semáne thántu, let them be.

Indefinite Tense.

Person — Singular.

1st ମୁ ଥାନ୍ତି mu thánti, I could be.

2nd ତୁ ଥାନ୍ତୁ tu thántu, thou wouldst be.

3rd ସେ ଥାନ୍ତା se thántá, he would be.

Plural.

1st ଆମ୍ଭେ ଥାନ୍ତୁ ámbhe thántu, we would be.

2nd ତୁମ୍ଭେ ଥାନ୍ତ tumbhe thánto, ye would be.

3rd ସେମାନେ ଥାନ୍ତେ semáne thánte, they would be.

Present verbal participle ଥାଉ tháu, being.

Past verbal participle ଥାଇ thái, having been.

Present relative participle ଥିବା thibá, which is, or will be.

Past relative participle ଥିଲା thilá, which was.

The auxiliary verb ହୋଇବାର hóibáro, or ହେବାର hebáro, to be or to become, is thus conjugated

Present Tense.

Person — Singular.

1st ମୁ ହୋଉଛି mu hóuchhi, I become.

2nd ତୁ ହୋଉଛୁ tu hóuts-hu, thou becomest.

3rd ସେ ହୋଉଛି se hóuchhi (com. héuchhi) he becomes.

Plural.

1st ଆମ୍ଭେ ହୋଉଛୁ ámbhe hóuts-hu, we become.

2nd ତୁମ୍ଭେ ହୋଉଛ tumbhe houts-ho, ye become.

3rd ସେମାନେ ହୋଉଛନ୍ତି semáne hóuts-honti, they become.

Past Tense.

Person Singular.

1st ମୁ ହୋଇଲି or ହେଲି mu heli, I became.
2nd ତୁ ହେଲୁ tu helu, thou becamest.
3rd ସେ ହେଲା se helá, he became.

Plural.

1st ଆମ୍ଭେ ହେଲୁ ámbhe helu, we became.
2nd ତୁମ୍ଭେ ହେଲ tumbhe helo, ye became.
3rd ସେମାନେ ହେଲେ semáne hele, they became.

Future Tense.

Person Singular.

1st ମୁ ହୋଇବି or ହେବି mu hebi, I shall become.
2nd ତୁ ହେବୁ tu hebu, thou shalt become.
3rd ସେ ହେବ se hebo, he will become.

Plural.

1st ଆମ୍ଭେ ହେବୁ ámbhe hebu, we will become.
2nd ତୁମ୍ଭେ ହେବ tumbhe hebo, ye will become.
3rd ସେମାନେ ହେବେ semáne hebe, they will become.

Imperative.

Become.

Person Singular.

1st ମୁ ହୋଏ mu hóe, let me become.
2nd ତୁ ହୋ tu hó, become.
3rd ସେ ହୋଉ se hóu, let him become.

Plural.

1st ଆମ୍ଭେ ହୋଉ ámbhe hóu, let us become.
2nd ତୁମ୍ଭେ ହୁଅ tumbhe huo, become.
3rd ସେମାନେ ହୁଅନ୍ତୁ semane huontu, let them become.

Indefinite Tense.

Person — Singular.

1st ମୁ ହୁଅନ୍ତି mu huonti, I would become.

2nd ତୁ ହୁଅନ୍ତୁ tu huontu, thou wouldst become.

3rd ସେ ହୁଅନ୍ତା se huontá, he would become.

Plural.

1st ଆମ୍ଭେ ହୁଅନ୍ତୁ ámbhe huontu, we would become.

2nd ତୁମ୍ଭେ ହୁଅନ୍ତ tumbhe huonto, ye would become.

3rd ସେମାନେ ହୁଅନ୍ତେ semáne huonte, they would become.

Present verbal participle ହୋଉ hóu or ହେଉ héu, becoming.

Past verbal participle ହୋଇ hói, having become.

Future relative participle ହେବା hebá, which becomes.

Past relative participle ହେଲା helá, which became.

The active verb କରିବାର koribáro, to do or make, is conjugated as follows :—

Present Tense.

I do.

Person — Singular.

1st ମୁ କରୁଅଛି mu koru-ochhi, I am doing, or I make.

2nd ତୁ କରୁଅଛୁ tu koru-otshu, thou art doing.

3rd ସେ କରୁଅଛି se koru-ochhi, he is doing.

Plural.

1st ଆମ୍ଭେ କରୁଅଛୁ ámbhe koru-otshu, we are doing.

2nd ତୁମ୍ଭେ କରୁଅଛ tumbhe koru-otsho, ye are doing.

3rd ସେମାନେ କରୁଅଛନ୍ତି semáne koru-otshonti, they are doing.

The present tense is usually contracted into ମୁ କରୁଛି mu koruchhi, ତୁ କରୁଛୁ tu korutshu, ସେ କରୁଛି se koruchhi, &c., I do, thou doest, he does, &c.

Past Tense.

Person — Singular.

1st ମୁ କରିଲି or କଲି mu koli, I did or made.
2nd ତୁ କଲୁ tu kolu, thou didst.
3rd ସେ କଲା se kolá, he did.

Plural.

1st ଅମ୍ଭେ କଲୁ ámbhe kolu, we did.
2nd ତୁମ୍ଭେ କଲ tumbhe kolo, ye did.
3rd ସେମାନେ କଲେ semáne kole, they did.

Future Tense.

Person — Singular.

1st ମୁ କରିବି mu koribi, I will do.
2nd ତୁ କରିବୁ tu koribu, thou wilt do.
3rd ସେ କରିବ se koribo, he will do.

Plural.

1st ଅମ୍ଭେ କରିବୁ ámbhe koribu, we will do.
2nd ତୁମ୍ଭେ କରିବ tumbhe koribo, ye will do.
3rd ସେମାନେ କରିବେ semáne koribe, they will do.

Imperative.

Person — Singular.

1st ମୁ କରେ mu kore, let me do.
2nd ତୁ କରେ tu kore, do thou.
3rd ସେ କରୁ se koru, let him do.

Person — Plural.

1st ଆମ୍ଭେ କରୁ ámbhe koru, let us do.
2nd ତୁମ୍ଭେ କର tumbhe koro, do ye.
3rd ସେମାନେ କରନ୍ତୁ semáne korontu, let them do.

Singular.

1st ମୁ କରନ୍ତି mu koronti, I would do.
2nd ତୁ କରନ୍ତୁ tu korontu, thou wouldst do.
3rd ସେ କରନ୍ତା se korontá, he would do.

Plural.

1st ଆମ୍ଭେ କରନ୍ତୁ ámbhe korontu, we would do.
2nd ତୁମ୍ଭେ କରନ୍ତ tumbhe koronto, ye would do.
3rd ସେମାନେ କରନ୍ତେ semáne koronte, they would do.

Present verbal participle — କରୁ koru, doing.
Past verbal participle — କରି kori, having done.
Future relative participle — କରିବା koribá, who does or will do.
Past relative participle — କଲା kolá, who or which did.

The formation of compound tenses is effected by means of the auxiliary verb ଥିବାର Thibáro, to be, and is as simple as the other parts of the Uriya verb:—

ମୁ କରୁଅଛି mu koru-ochhi, I am doing.
ମୁ କରିଅଛି mu kori-ochhi, I have done.
ମୁ କରୁଥିଲି mu koru-thili, I was doing.
ମୁକରିଥିଲି mu kori-thili, I had done.
ମୁ କରୁଥିବି mu koru-thibi, I shall be doing.
ମୁ କରିଥିବି mu kori-thibi, I shall have done.
ମୁ କରୁ ଥାଏ mu koru-tháe, I am in the habit of doing.
ମୁ କରି ଥାଏ mu kori-tháe, I used to do.

ମୁ କରୁଥିଲେ mu koru-thile, if I were doing.
ମୁ କରିଥିଲେ mu kori-thile, if I had done.
ମୁ କରୁଥାନ୍ତି mu koru-thánti, I would be doing.
ମୁ କରିଥାନ୍ତି mu kori-thánti, I would have done.

The use of the RELATIVE PARTICIPLE in Uriya is peculiar. It is formed by adding to the past verbal participle of the verb the termination ବା bá for the present tense, and ଲା lá for the past. Examples:

Present.

ମୁ ଦେବା ଧାନ mu debá dháno, lit. I, which give, the corn, or, The corn which I give.

Past.

ମୁ ଦେଲା ଟଙ୍କା mu delá ṭonká, lit. I, which gave, the rupee, or, The rupee which I gave.

Progr. present.

ମୁ ଦେଉଥିବା ଟଙ୍କା mu deu-thibá ṭonká, lit. I, which am giving, the rupee, or, The rupee which I am giving.

Progr. Past.

ମୁ ଦେଇଥିବା ଟଙ୍କା mu dei-thibá ṭonká, lit. I, which have given, the rupee, or, The rupee which I have given.

THE PASSIVE VOICE in Uriya is formed by adding to the passive participle of the verb, either the auxiliary verb ହେବାର hebáro, to become, or the irregular verb ଯିବାର jibáro, to go.

The PASSIVE PARTICIPLE is formed by adding ଆ a to the root of the verb, as ଦେଖ dekho, see, becomes ଦେଖା dekhá, seen. EXAMPLE, ସେ ଦେଖା ହେଲା Se dekhá helá the usual form, or ସେ ଦେଖା ଗଲା Se dekhá golá, he was seen.

If, however, the root of the verb ends in ଏ e, this vowel must be changed into ଇ i before the passive affix ଆ á, as in ଦେ de, give, which becomes ଦିଆ diá, given.

In like manner when the root of the verb ends either in ଆ á, or in ଓ ó, the passive participle is formed by changing these two vowels into ଉ u before the passive affix ଆ á thus ଖା kha, eat, becomes ଖୁଆ khuá, eaten, and ଧୋ dhó, wash, becomes ଧୁଆ dhuá, washed. Whilst ମାର máro, beat, becomes ମରା morá, beaten.

THE VERB ଯିବାର jibáro, to go, is irregular and is declined as follows :—

PRESENT TENSE.

Person	Singular.
1st	ମୁ ଯାଉଛି mu jáuchhi, I go.
2nd	ତୁ ଯାଉଛୁ tu jáuts-hu, thou goest.
3rd	ସେ ଯାଉଛି se jáuchhi, he goes.

Person	Plural.
1st	ଆମ୍ଭେ ଯାଉଛୁ ámbhe jáuts-hu, we go.
2nd	ତୁମ୍ଭେ ଯାଉଛ tumbhe jáuts-ho, you go.
3rd	ସେମାନେ ଯାଉଛନ୍ତି semáne jáuts-honti, they go.

Past Tense.

Person	Singular.
1st	ମୁ ଗଲି mu goli, I went.
2nd	ତୁ ଗଲୁ tu golu, thou wentest.
3rd	ସେ ଗଲା se golá, he went.

Person	Plural.
1st	ଆମ୍ଭେ ଗଲୁ ámbhe golu, we went.
2nd	ତୁମ୍ଭେ ଗଲ tumbhe golo, you went.
3rd	ସେ ମାନେ ଗଲେ semáne gole, they went.

Future Tense.

ମୁ ଯିବି mu jibi, I will go.
ଆମ୍ଭେ ଯିବୁ ámbhe jibu, we will go.

Conditional.

ମୁ ଯାନ୍ତି mu jánti, I would go.
ଆମ୍ଭେ ଯାନ୍ତୁ ámbhe jántu, we would go, etcetera.

Present	v.	part.	ଯାଉ jáu, going.
Past	v.	part.	ଯାଇ jái, having gone.
Pres.	rel.	part.	ଯିବା jibá, who or which goes.
Past	rel.	part.	ଗଲା golá, who or which went.

Lastly, causal verbs in Uriya are formed by adding ଆ á to the root of the verb, as in the passive voice, and adding to the passive participle the termination ଇବାର ibáro.

Example: ଦେଖିବାର dekhibáro, to see, becomes ଦେଖାଇବାର dekháibáro, to cause to see *i. e.* to show

ଦେବାର debáro, to give becomes ଦିଆଇବାର diáibáro, to cause to give.

ଖାଇବାର kháibáro, to eat, becomes ଖୁଆଇବାର khuáibáro, to cause to eat *i. e.* to feed.

ଆଣିବାର áṇibáro,to bring, becomes ଅଣାଇବାର oṇáibáro to cause to bring, *i. e.* to fetch, and ଡାକବାର ḍákibáro, to call, becomes ଡକାଇବାର ḍokáibáro, to cause to call *i. e.* to summon.

PART THE SECOND.

DIALOGUES IN ENGLISH, URIYA AND ROMAN CHARACTER.

INTRODUCTORY.

I.

DIALOGUES.

INTRODUCTORY.	କଥାବାର୍ତ୍ତାରମ୍ଭ ।	KOTHÁBÁRTTÁROMBHO.
ENGLISH.	URIYA.	ROMAN.
Who are you?	ତୁ କେସେ ?	Tu kése?
I am a cooly.	ମୁ ମୂଲିଆ ।	Mu muliá.
What do you want?	ତୋତେ କଣ ଲୋଡ଼ା ?	Tóte kono lóḍá?
I want nothing.	ମୋତେ କିଛି ଲୋଡ଼ା ନାହିଁ ।	Móte kichhi lóḍá náhiṇ.
Be silent.	ତୁନି ରହ ।	Tuni roho.
Take care.	ଜାଗ୍ରତ କର ।	Dzágroto koro.
Don't make a noise.	ତୁଣ୍ଡ କର ନା ।	Tundo koro ná.
Shut the door.	କବାଟ ପକା ।	Kobáṭo poká.
Open the door.	କବାଟ କାଢ଼ି ଦେ ।	Kobáṭo káḍhi de.
It is very late.	ବଡ଼ ଉଚ୍ଛୁର ହେଲା ।	Boḍo uts-tshoro helá.
It is not yet nine o'clock.	ଆଉର ନ ଘଣ୍ଟା ହୋଇ ନାହିଁ ।	A'uri no ghoṇṭo hói náhiṇ.
Tell the truth, don't tell lies.	ସତ କହ, ମିଛ କହ ନା ।	Soto koho, mits-ho koho ná.
Where is my horse?	ଆମର ଘୋଡ଼ା କୋଠାରେ ?	A'moro ghóḍá kóṭháre?

It is in the village.	ଗାଁରେ ଅଛି ।	Gáṇre ochhi.
Who went to fetch my horse?	ମୋର ଘୋଡ଼ା ଆଣିବାକୁ କେସେ ଗଲା ?	Móro ghóḍá áṇibáku kése golá ?
No one went.	କେ ଗଲା ନାହିଁ ।	Ké golá náhiṇ.
Will you go?	ଯିବୁ କି ?	Jibu-ki ?
I will go.	ମୁ ଯିବି ।	Mu jibi.
Why did he go?	ସେ କାହିଁକି ଗଲା ?	Se káhiṇki golá ?
I do not know.	ମୋତେ ଜଣା ନାହିଁ ।	Móte dzoṇá náhiṇ.
Why did he come?	ସେ କାହିଁକି ଆସିଲା ?	Sẹ káhiṇki ásilá ?
Who is coming?	କେସେ ଆସୁଛି ?	Kése asuchhi ?
A man is coming along the road.	ମନୁଷ୍ୟ ବାଟରେ ଆସୁଛି ।	Monushyo baṭore asuchhi.
I see a man coming along the road.	ମନୁଷ୍ୟ ବାଟରେ ଆସିବାର ମୁ ଦେଖୁଛି ।	Monushyo báṭore ásibáro mu dekhuchhi.
What is the name of the man coming along the road?	ବାଟରେ ଆସୁଥିବା ମନୁଷ୍ୟର ନାମ କଣ ?	Báṭore ásu-thibá monushyoro námo koṇo ?
Call him.	ତାକୁ ଡାକି ଦେ ।	Táku ḍáki de.

English.	Uriya.	Roman.
Tell him to come quickly.	ବେଗି ଅସିବାର ଅଛି ତାକୁ କହିଦେ ।	Bégi ásibáro ochhi táku kohi de.
When will you come? (plur.)	ତୁମେ କେବେ ଅସିବ ?	Tume kebe ásibo?
We will come to-morrow.	ଅମେ କାଲି ଅସିବୁ ।	A'me káli ásibu.
I have no work, and have come to see you.	ମୋର କିଛି ପାଇଟି ନ ଥିବାରୁ ତୁମର ଦର୍ଶନକୁ ଅସିଅଛି ।	Móro kichhi páiṭi no thibáru tumoro dors'onoku ási-ochhi.
If you had come before, I should have seen you.	ତୁ ଅଗେ ଅସି ଥିଲେ ତୋତେ ଦେଖି ଥାନ୍ତି	Tu áge ási-thile tóte dekhi-thánti.
If they had come before, he would have seen them.	ସେମାନେ ଅଗେ ଅସିଥିଲେ ସେ ତାଙ୍କୁ ଦେଖିଥାନ୍ତା ।	Sémáne áge ási-thile se táṅg-ku dekhi-thántá.
Iron is heavy.	ଲୁହା ଭାରି ହୋଇ ଅଛି ।	Luhá bhári hói-ochhi.
Silver is heavier.	ରୁପା ତାକୁ ପ୍ରତି ଭାରି ହୋଇଅଛି ।	Rúpá táku proti bhári hói-ochhi.
Gold is the heaviest.	ସୁନା ସମସ୍ତଙ୍କ ପ୍ରତି ଭାରି ହୋଇଅଛି ।	Suná somostongko proti bhári hói-ochhi.

Wood is light.	କାଠ ଉସ୍ୱାସ ହୋଇଅଛି ।	Káṭho uswáso hói-ochhi.
Cotton is lighter.	କପା ଢାଲୁ ପ୍ରତି ଉସ୍ୱାସ ହୋଇଅଛି ।	Kopá táku próti uswáso hói-ochhi.
A feather is lightest.	ପକ୍ଷୀ ସମସ୍ତଙ୍କ ପ୍ରତି ଉସ୍ୱାସ ହୋଇଅଛି ।	Pokhi somostongko proti uswáso hói-ochhi.
Bring the eggs which I bought to-day.	ମୁ ଆଜି କିଣିବା ଡିମ୍ବ ଆଣେ ।	Mu áji kiṇibá ḍimbo áṇe.
The rice which you sell is not good.	ତୁ ବିକିବା ଚାଉଳ ଭଲ ନାହିଁ ।	Tu bikibá tsáuḷo bholo náhiñ.
The rice which he bought yesterday was good.	ସେ କାଲି କିଣିଥିବା ଚାଉଳ ଭଲ ହୋଇ ଥିଲା ।	Se káli kiṇi-thibá tsáuḷo bholo hói-thilá.
Milk the cow.	ଗାଈଠାରୁ ଦୁଧ ଦୁହେଁ ।	Gáiṭháru dudho duheñ.
Ghee is obtained by cooking butter.	ଲହୁଣିକି ରାନ୍ଧିଲେ ଘିଅ ବାହାରିବ ।	Lohuṇiki rándhile ghio báhá-ribo.
There is no cream on this milk, you have been mixing water in it.	ଏ ଦୁଧରେ ସର ନାହିଁ ତହିଁରେ ପାଣି ମିସାଇ ଦେଲୁ ।	E dudhore soro náhiṇ tohiñre páṇi misái delu.

English.	Uriya.	Roman.
Are there any letters for me?	ଅମର ନାମରେ କି ହେଲେ ଚିଠାଉ ଅଛୁ କି ?	A′moro námore ki hele chiṭáu-ochhiki?
When does the post leave?	ଟପା କେତେ ଘଣ୍ଟାକୁ ଯିବ ?	Ṭopá kete ghonṭoku jibo?
Go and enquire at what o'clock the post leaves.	ଟପା କେତେ ଘଣ୍ଟାକୁ ଯିବ ବୋଲି ବୁଝି ଅସେ ।	Ṭopá kete ghonṭoku jibo bóli bujhi áse.
Change this rupee and bring me a quarter of a rupee, four two-anna pieces, and the rest in copper.	ଟଙ୍କାଟି ଭଙ୍ଗାଇ କରି ଗୋଟିଏ ଶୁକି ଚ୍ୱରଟା ଦୁଅଣି ଆଉ ବାକି ପଇଶା ମୋଟେ ଅଣି ଦେ ।	E ṭonkáṭi bhongái kori góṭie s′úki tsáriṭá dioṇi áu báki pois′á móte áṇi de.
When that gentleman received from you the letter which I sent, and said that he himself would come to-morrow, why did you not ask by which road, and at what time, he was coming?	ସେ ସାହେବ ଆମେ ପଠାଇଲା ଚିଠାଉ ତୋଠାରୁ ନେଇ କାଲିକି ସେ ଆପେ ଆସିବେ ବୋଲି କହିଲା ବେଳେ ସେ କୋ ବାଟରେ ଆସିବେ କି କେତେ-ବେଳେ ଆସିବେ କି ତୁ କାହିଁକି ପଚ୍ଛରିଲୁ ନାହିଁ?	Se sáhebo áme poṭháilá chiṭáu tóṭháru néi káliki se ápe ásibe bóli kohilá beḷe, se kó báṭore ásibeki, kete beḷe ásibeki, tu káhiñki potsárilu náhiñ?

Call the man who brought this letter from the other side of the river, and tell him that I will send an answer to the gentleman at ½ past 6 o'clock this evening.	ନଦୀ ସେ ପାଖରୁ ଏ ଚିଠାଉ ଅଣିଲା ମନୁଷ୍ୟକୁ ଡାକି କରି କହ ଯେ ଆମେ ଆଜି ସନ୍ଧ୍ୟା ଛ ଘଣ୍ଟା ଅଧେ ସମୟରେ ସାହେବଙ୍କୁ ଜବାବ ପଠାଇବା ।	Nodí se pákhoru é chiṭáu áṇilá monushyoku ḍákikori koho je áme áji sondhiyá ts-ho ghonṭo odhe somoyore sáhebongku dzobábo poṭháibá.
Run quickly to the Agent's house and inquire whether any of the gentlemen who landed from the steamer at day-break, have brought letters or parcels for me or not?	ତୁ ଏଜେଣ୍ଟ ସାହେବଙ୍କର ଘରକୁ ବେଗେ (ବେଗି) ଧାଇଁ ଯାଇ କାଲି ଧୂଆ ବୋଇତ ଉପରୁ ଓହ୍ଲାଇଲା ସାହେବମାନଙ୍କରେ କେସେ ହେଲେ ଆମର ନାମରେ ଚିଠାଉ ଅବା ବୁଜୁଳା ଆଣିଲେ କି ନାହିଁ ତାହା ବୁଝି ଆସେ ।	Tu "Agent" sáhebongkoro ghoroku bege (com. bégi) dháiñ jái káli dhúá bóito uporu óhláilá sáhebománongkore kése hele ámoro námore chiṭáu obá budzuḷá áṇileke náhiñ táhá bujhi ásé?

ON CULTIVATION.

II.

ON CULTIVATION.	ଚାଷ କରିବା ବିଷୟ ।	TSÁSO KORIBA BISHOYO.
ENGLISH.	URIYA.	ROMAN.
What is your occupation ?	ତୋର କି ବୃତ୍ତି ?	Tóro ki brutti ?
My occupation is farming.	ମୋର ବୃତ୍ତି ଚାଷ (com. ତାସ) ।	Móro brutti tsáso (com. táso).
What is the name of your village ?	ତୋର କୋ ଗ୍ରାମ ?	Tóro kó grámo ? (idiomatically).
State why you have presented a petition.	ତୁ କାହିଁକି ଅର୍ଜି ଦାଖଲ କରୁଅଛୁ ତାହା କହ ?	Tu káhiñki orji dákholo koruotshu táhá koho ?
Nothing has ripened this year on my land.	ଏ ବର୍ଷ ମୋ ଭୂମିରେ କିଛି ପାଚିଲା ନାହିଁ ?	E borsho mó bhúmire kichhi páchilá náhiñ.
Nevertheless I have paid half my rent out of my house-	ତଥାପି ଏ ସରିକି ମୋ ଘର ଅସ୍ତିରୁ ଅଧେ ଟଙ୍କା ବାନ୍ଧିଲି, ଅଉ ହଲ ଯୋ-	Tothápi e soriki mó ghoro ástiru odhé ṭonká bándhili

hold property and have only two pairs of bullocks left.	ଢ଼ିବ ମାତ୍ର ଅଛୁ ।	áu holo jóḍie mátro ochhi.
The village Karnam and the Karji are demanding the rest of the rent	ଗ୍ରାମ କରଣ କାର୍ଯି ବାକ ଟଙ୍କା ମାଗୁଛନ୍ତି ।	Grámo koroṇo kárji báki ṭonká mágutshonti.
I have nothing left of my property.	ମୋର ଆଉ କଛୁ ଅସ୍ତି ନାହିଁ ।	Móro áu kichhi ásti náhin.
How am I to pay the rest of the money?	ବାକ ଟଙ୍କା କ ରୂପେ ଦେବ ?	Báki ṭonká ki rúpe debi ?
What crops have ripened this year on your land?	ଏ ବର୍ଷ ତୋ ଭୂମିରେ କ କ ଜନସ ପାଚିଲା ?	E borsho tó bhúmire ki ki jiniso páchilá ?
In all two bharnums of paddy ripened on my wet land.	ମୋର ବଲରେ ଧାନ ସବୁ ଦୁଇ ଭରଣ ପାଚିଲା ।	Móro bilore dháno sobu dui bhoroṇo páchilá.
On the dry land gingely raggi and other grains ripened to the amount of twenty-two rupees.	ପଦରରେ ରାଶି ମାଣ୍ଡିଆ ଅଗେର ବାଇଶି ଟଙ୍କାର ପାଚିଲା ।	Podorore rás'i máṇḍiá ogáirá báis'i ṭonkáro páchilá.

English.	Uriya.	Roman.
What is the amount of your rent?	ତୋର ଗୁତା ସବୁ କେତେ ?	Tóro gutá sobu kete ?
My rent is about one hundred and twenty rupees.	ମୋର ଗୁତା ଶଏ୍ କୋଡ଼ିଏ ଟଙ୍କା ହେବ ।	Móro gutá s'oye kóḍie ṭonká hebo.
I did not even obtain a full crop last year.	ଗତ ସାଲରେ ମଧ୍ୟ ମୋ ଭୂମି ପୁରା ପାଚିଲା ନାହିଁ ।	Goto sálore modhyo mo bhumi púrá páchilá náhiñ.
I only received eighteen rupees remission for my losses.	ନଷ୍ଟି ପାଇଁ ମାଠ ·ଠାରଶି ଟଙ୍କା ମାଫ ପାଇଁ ପାଇ ଅଛି ।	Noshṭi páiṇ matro oṭhais'i ṭonka mapho paiṇ paï ochhi.
How many pairs of bullocks have you?	ତୋର କେତେ ହଳ ବଳଦ ଅଛି ?	Tóro kete hoḷo boḷodo ochhi ?
I have two pairs of bullocks and three pairs of female buffaloes.	ମୋର ଦୁଇ ହଳ ବଳଦ ତିନି ହଳ ମହିଷୀ ଅଛି ।	Móro dui hoḷo boḷodo tini hoḷo mohinshí ochhi.
What are you looking for?	କଣ ଖୋଜୁଛୁ ?	Koṇo khódzutshu ?
I have lost my bullock.	ମୋର ବଳଦ ହଜିଗଲା ।	Móro boḷodo hóji-golá.

Have you not yet found your bullock?	ତୋତେ ବଳଦ ଅଉର ଦଶି ନାହିଁ କି ?	Tóte boḷodo áuri dis'i náhiñ-ki?
See there is a buffalo grazing.	ହେଟି ଗୋଟିଏ ପୋଢ଼ ଚରୁଛି ।	Héti! góṭie póḍho tsoruchhi.
I drove the calf off the field, and placed it in the pound.	ବାଛୁରିକି ମୋର ବିଲୁରୁ କାଢ଼ି ଦେଇ ମୁ ଦୋଡ଼ିରେ ରଖିଲି?	Bátshuriki móro biloru káḍhi dei mu dóḍire rokhili.
How many cows have you in your herd?	ତୋର ଗୋଠରେ କେତେ ଗାଇ ଅଛି?	Tóro góṭhore kete gái ochhi?
The herdsman drives the cows daily out to graze.	ଜଗୁଆଳି ପ୍ରତି ଦିନ ଗାଇକି ଚରାଉଛି ।	Dzoguáli proti dino gáiki tsoráuchhi.
Have you any goats for sale?	ବିକିବାକୁ ତୋଠାରେ ଛେଳି ଅଛି କି?	Bikibáku tóṭháre chheḷi och-hiki?
No, they all died last year owing to continuous rain.	ନାହିଁ ଗଲା ବର୍ଷରେ ଝଡ଼ି କରିବାରୁ ସବୁ ମରି ଗଲେ ।	Náhiṇ, golá borshore jhoḍi koribáru sobu mori-gole.
A flood came down the river and did much damage.	ନଦୀ ବଢ଼ି ଆସିକରି ବହୁତ ନାଶ ହୋଇ ଗଲା ।	Nodí boḍhi ási-kori bohuto nás'o hói-golá.
Our fields are all swamped.	ଆମର ବିଲମାନଙ୍କରେ ପାଣି ଭର୍ତ୍ତି ହୋଇ ଅଛି	A'moro bilománongkore páṇí bhortti kori hói-ochhi.

ENGLISH.	URIYA.	ROMAN.
The crops are all burnt up.	ଖନ୍ଦମାନେ ସବୁ ପୋଡ଼ି ଗଲେ।	Khondománe sobu póḍi-gole
How is cotton looking?	କପା କିରୂପେ ଅଛି।	Kopá kirúpe ochhi?
Has the raggy not yet been cut?	ମାଣ୍ଡିଆ କଟା ହେଲା କି ନାହିଁ?	Máṇḍiyá koṭa ɦelá-ki náhiñ?
When will you cultivate your fields?	ବିଲ କେବେ ଚାଷ କରିବ?	Bilo kebe tsáso (com. táso) koribo?
We shall cultivate it in another two months, if it rains.	ଦୁଇ ମାସ ଗଲେ ପାଣି ବର୍ଷିଲେ ଚାଷ କରିବୁ।	Dui máso gole páṇi borshile tsáso koribu.
The ground is not yet soft enough for the plough.	ହଳ ବାନ୍ଧିବାକୁ ଭୂମି ଏବେ ବତର ନାହିଁ।	Hoḷo bándhibáku bhúmi ebe botoro náhiñ.
Why have you not cultivated this waste land?	ଏ ପଡ଼ିଆ ଭୂମି ତୁମେ କାହିଁକି ଉଠିଆ କଲ ନାହିଁ?	E poḍiyá bhúmi tume káhiñki uṭhiá kolo náhiñ?

We have not cultivated it as the soil is not good.	ଭୂମି ଉତ୍ତମ ନ ଥିବାରୁ ଉଠିଆ କଲୁ ନାହିଁ ।	Bhúmi uttomo, no thibáru uṭhiá kolu náhiñ.
When will the paddy be ripe?	ଧାନ କେବେ ପାଚିବ ?	Dháno kebe páchibo?
If the weather remains fine it will be cut in another seven days.	କାଲ ଭଲ ହୋଇଥିଲେ ଆଉ ସାତ ଦିନରେ କଟା ହେବ ।	Káḷo bholo hói-thile áu sáto dinore koṭá hebo.
When will you transplant the young paddy plants?	ଧାନ ତଲି ଭାଙ୍ଗି କରି କେବେ ରୋଇବ ?	Dháno toḷi bhángi kori kebe róibo?
The grain ripens two months after transplanting the young plants.	ତଲି ରୋଇଲା ଉତ୍ତାରୁ ଧାନ ଦୁଇ ମାସ-ଠାରେ ପାଚିବ ।	Toḷi róilá uttáru dháno dui másoṭháre páchibo.
What seed have you sown in your field?	ତୋର ବିଲରେ କି ବିହନ ବୁଣିଥିଲୁ ?	Tóro bilore ki bihono buṇi-thilu?
I have sown castor oil seed.	ମୁ କାଲ ବୁଣି ଥିଲି ।	Mu kálo buni-thili.
Why has the gardener not sown the seeds I gave him in the garden?	ମାଲିକ ଆମେ ଦେବା ମଞ୍ଜି ସେ ତୋଟାରେ କାହିଁକି ଲଗାଇଲା ନାହିଁ ।	Máliki áme debá monji se tóṭáre káhiñki logáilá náhiñ?

English.	Uriya.	Roman.
The seed which we planted has all come up.	ଯେଉଁ ମଞ୍ଜି ଆମେ ଲଗାଇଲୁ ସେ ସବୁ ଗଛ ହୋଇ ଗଲା ।	Jéuṇ monji áme logáilu se sobu gotsho hói-golá.
What crops are there in your village?	ତୋର ଗାଁରେ କି କି ଖନ୍ଦ ହୋଇଅଛି ?	Tóro gáñre ki ki khondo hói-ochhi?
Do they cultivate sugar-cane?	ଆଖୁ କରୁଛନ୍ତି-କି ?	A'khu korutshonti-ki?
The ryots came in the night time and out of enmity cut the bund of our tank.	ରଇତମାନେ ଅମ୍ଭଠାରେ ଈର୍ଷା କରି ରାତିରେ ଆସି କରି ଆମର ବନ୍ଧ ହାଣି ଦେଲେ ।	Roitománe ámbhoṭháre írshá kori rátire ási-kori ámoro bondho háṇi deḷe.
If it does not rain, there will be a famine.	ପାଣି ନ ବର୍ଷିଲେ ମହର୍ଗ ହେବ ।	Páṇi no borshile mohorgo hebo.
As there has been no rain, the tank has dried up.	ବର୍ଷା ନ ବର୍ଷିବାରୁ ବନ୍ଧ ଶୁଖିଗଲା ।	Borshá no borshibáru bondho sukhi-golá.
As there has been no rain in the village, the crops have all been burnt up.	ସେ ଗାଁରେ ପାଣି ନ ବର୍ଷିବାରୁ ଖନ୍ଦ ସବୁ ପୋଡ଼ିଗଲା ।	Se gáñre páṇi no borshibáru khondo sobu póḍi-golá.

If the ryots want water, they must dig wells.	ରଇତମାନଙ୍କୁ ପାଣି ଲୋଡ଼ା ହେଲେ ସେମାନେ କୁହଁ ଖୋଳିବାର ଅଛି ।	Roitománongku páṇi lóḍá hele sémáne kuhoñ khóḷibáro ochhi.
If they had dug wells, the crops would have been saved.	ସେମାନେ କୁହଁ ଖୋଳିଥିଲେ ଖନ୍ଦ ସବୁ ହୋଇଥାନ୍ତା ।	Sémáne kuhoñ khóḷithile khondo sobu hói-thántá.
Is there any cattle disease in the village?	ଏ ଗାଁରେ ଗୋରୁମାନଙ୍କୁ କି ଅବା ରୋଗ ଜାତ ହୋଇଅଛି କି ?	E gáñre górumánongku ki obá rógo dzáto hói-ochhiki?
The indigo which the ryots have sown looks well.	ତସାମାନେ ବୁଣିଥିବା ନୀଳି ଖନ୍ଦ ଭଲ କରି ଦିଶୁଛି ।	Tosámáne buṇi-thibá níḷi khondo bholo kori disuchhi.
As the crop is deficient the money-lender will not give credit.	ଖନ୍ଦ ଊଣା ହେବାରୁ ସାହୁକାର ପ୍ରତ୍ୟୟ କରୁ ନାହିଁ ।	Khondo uṇá hebáru sáhukáro protyoyo koru náhiñ.
If therefore you will give me time I will put down a fresh crop, and pay the money.	ଏ ସକାଶରୁ କିଛି ହେଲେ ବାଇଦା ଦେଲେ ଫେରେ ଖନ୍ଦ କରି ଟଙ୍କା ବାନ୍ଧି ଦେବି ।	E sokás'oru kichhi hele báidá dele phere khondo kori ṭonká bándhi debi.

ON CUTCHERRY.

III.

ON CUTCHERRY.	କଚେରି ବିଷୟ ।	KOCHERI BISHOYO.
ENGLISH.	URIYA.	ROMAN.
What is your name ?	ତୋର ନାମ କଣ ?	Tóro námo kono ?
What trade do you practise ?	ତୁ କି ବୃତ୍ତି କରୁଛୁ ?	Tu ki brutti korutshu ?
I am a blacksmith.	ମୁଁ କମାର ।	Mu komáro.
How old are you ?	ତୋତେ କେତେ ବୟସ ହେବ	Tóte kete boyoso hebo ?
I am twenty years old.	ମୋତେ କୋଡ଼ିଏ ବର୍ଷ ହେଲା ।	Móte kóḍie borsho helá.
Where do you live ?	ତୁ କୋଠାରେ ଅଛୁ ?	Tu kóṭháre ots-hu ?
Speak out. What do you want ?	ଅଣ୍ଟ କରି କହ ତୋତେ କଣ ଲୋଡ଼ା ?	Anṭo kori koho. Tóte koṇo lóḍá ?
These two persons were fighting in the street.	ଏ ଦୁଇ ଜଣ ସାଇରେ ମାଡ଼ଗୋଳ ହୋଇ ଥିଲେ ।	E dui dzoṇo sáire máḍo-góḷo hói-thile.

About 6 months ago a theft took place in my house.	ରମାରମୀ ଛ ମାସ ହେଲା ମୋର ଘରେ ଗୋଟିଏ ଚୋରୀ ହୋଇଥିଲା ।	Romáromí tsho máso helá móro ghore, góṭie tsórí hóithilá.
Did you make a complaint at the time before the village moonsiff?	ସେ କାଳରେ ତୁ ଗାଁ କାର୍ଯୀଠାରେ ଫିର୍ୟାଦ କରିଥିଲୁ କି ?	Se káḷore tu gáñ kárjíṭháre phiryádo kori-thiluki?
What offence have they committed?	ସେମାନେ କି ଦୋଷ କରିଅଛନ୍ତି ।	Semáne ki dósho kori-otshonti?
They made a hole in the mud-wall, and carried off all his things.	ବଇରେ ସିନ୍ଧ କରି କରି ସରଞ୍ଜାମ ଜାକ ଚୋରାଇ ଘେନିନେଲେ ।	Boire sindho kori kori sorondzámo dzáko tsórái gheni nele.
Swear in the witness.	ସାକ୍ଷୀକି ନିୟମ କରାଅ ।	Sákhíki niyámo koráo.
He took a stick and hit him on the head with it.	ଗୋଟିଏ ବାଡ଼ି ଧରି ତାର ମୁଣ୍ଡ ଉପରେ ପିଟିଦେଲା ।	Góṭie báḍi dhori táro munḍo upore piṭi delá.
From whom did you first of all obtain the land?	ପ୍ରଥମରେ ଏ ଭୂମି ତୋତେ କାହାଠାରୁ ପ୍ରାପ୍ତ ହେଲା ?	Prothomoreé bhúmi tóte káháṭháru prápto helá?

English.	Uriya.	Roman.
I saw him running away, but was unable to recognize him.	ସେ ପଳାଉଥିବାର ମୁ ଦେଖିଲି ତାକୁ ଚିହ୍ନି ନ ପାରିଲି ।	Se poḷáu-thibáro mu dekhili ni táku chihni no párili.
Who was there when you paid the money?	ତୁ ସେ ଟଙ୍କା ବାନ୍ଧିଲା ବେଳେ କେସେ ଥିଲା ?	Tu se ṭonká bándhilá beḷe kése thilá?
If you cheat in this way, you will be punished.	ଏ ପରି ଦଗା କଲେ ତୋତେ ଶିକ୍ଷା କରିବାକୁ ହେବ ।	E pori dogá kole tóte s'ikhyá koribáku hebo.
Was the chain on the door, or was it broken?	କବାଟରେ ସିଙ୍କୁଲି ଥିଲା କି ଭାଗି ଗଲା କି ?	Kobáṭore sinkuli thilá ki bhá-gi golá-ki?
He locked the door and brought me the key.	କବାଟ କୁଞ୍ଚି ପକାଇ ଦେଇ ସେ କୁଞ୍ଚିକାଠି ମୋତେ ଆଣି ଦେଲା ।	Kobáṭo kunchi pokái déi se kunchi-káṭhi móte áṇi-delá.
This case will take two or three days to finish.	ଏ ନମ୍ବର ଫଇସଲ କରିବାକୁ ଦୁଇ ଦିନ କି ତିନି ଦିନ ଲାଗିବ ।	E nomboro phoisolo koribáku dui dino ki tini dino lágibo.
Traces have been found which will lead to the prisoner's conviction.	ଏ କୈଦିକି ଶିକ୍ଷା ହେବା ପରି ହେତୁ ମିଳିଲା ।	E koidiki sikhyá hebá pori hétu mililá.

He was sentenced to 2 years' rigorous imprisonment.	ଦୁଇ ବର୍ଷ ପାଇଟି କରବା କୈଦରେ ରହବାକୁ ତାକୁ ତୀର୍ପୁ ହେଲା ।	Dui borsho páiṭi koribá koidire rohibáku táku tírpu helá.
The witnesses should not be examined within the hearing of one another, and in future examinations they must be kept apart.	ଅଗ ବିଚାରଣା କରବା ସମୟରେ ଗୋଟିଏ ସାକ୍ଷୀର ବିମର୍ଷା ଆଉ ଗୋଟିଏ ସାକ୍ଷୀ ନ ଶୁଣିଲା ପରି ସେ ସାକ୍ଷୀମାନଙ୍କୁ ଦୂରରେ ରଖିବାର ଅଛି ।	A'go bitsároṇá koribá somoyore góṭie sákhíro bimorshá áu góṭie sákhí no s'unilá pori se sákhímánongku dúrore rokhibáro ochhi.
If you weigh the silver, you will ascertain its value.	ଏ ରୂପାକୁ ତୁଳିଲେ କେତେ ଖରିଦ ହେବାର ଜଣା ପଡ଼ିବ ।	E rupáku tuḷile kete khorído hebáró dzoṇá poḍibo.
This watch is offered to me for 100 Rupees, shall I do right to buy it?	ଏ ଘଣ୍ଟା ଶଏ ଟଙ୍କାକୁ ବିକ ଦେବାକୁ ମୋତେ ଯାଚୁଛି ଯେ ଏ ଘଣ୍ଟା ରଖିଲେ ଭଲ କି ନାହିଁ ?	E ghonṭo soye ṭonkáku bikidebáku móte játsuchhi j e e ghonṭo rokhile bholo ki ná, hiñ ?
What proof have you that the party offering it came by it honestly.	ଏ ଘଣ୍ଟା ଯାଚୁଥିବା ଆସାମିକୁ ନ୍ୟାୟରେ ମିଳିଲା ପରି ତୋତେ କେମନ୍ତ ଜଣା ହେଲା ?	E ghonṭo játsu-thibá ásámiku nyáyore mililá pori tóte kémonto dzoṇá helá ?

ENGLISH.	URIYA.	ROMAN.
If he had offered it for a less sum, my suspicions would have been raised; but what he asks appears to be its full value.	ସେ ଘଣ୍ଟା ଯେବେ ମୋତେ ଊଣା ଖରିଦକୁ ଯାଚିଥାନ୍ତା ତେବେ ମୋତେ ସନ୍ଦେହ ହୁଅନ୍ତା ମାତ୍ର ଉଚିତ ଖରିଦ କହିବାରୁ ମୋତେ କିଛି ସନ୍ଦେହ ଲାଗୁ ନାହିଁ ।	Se ghonṭo jebe móte uṇá khorídoku jáchithántá, tebe móte sondého huontá, mátro uchito khorído kohibáru móte kichhi sondého lágu náhiñ.

ON READING AND WRITING.

IV.

ON READING AND WRITING.	ଲେଖା ପଢ଼ା ବିଷୟ ।	LEKHÁ POḌHÁ BISHOO.Y
ENGLISH.	URIYA.	ROMAN.
Can you read?	ପଢ଼ି ପାରୁଛୁକି ?	Poḍhi párutshu-ki?
I can read.	ମୋତେ ପାଠ ଆସୁଛି ।	Móte páṭho ásuchhi.
Can you write?	ଲେଖି ପାରୁଛୁକି ?	Lekhi párutshu-ki?
I cannot write.	ମୋତେ ଲେଖା ଆସୁ ନାହିଁ ?	Móte lékhá ásu náhiñ.
How long will it take to learn Uriya?	ଓଡ଼ିଆ ଶିଖିବାକୁ କେତେ କାଳ ଯିବ ?	O'ḍiyá s'ikhibáku kete káḷo jibo?
He knows Uriya well.	ତାହାକୁ ଓଡ଼ିଆ ଭଲ କରି ଆସୁଛି ।	Táháku óḍiyá bholo kori ásu-chhi.
If you speak Uriya thus, every body will understand you.	ଏ ପରି ଓଡ଼ିଆ କଥା କହିଲେ ସମସ୍ତେ ବୁଝି ପାରିବେ ।	E pori óḍiyá kothá kohile, somoste bujhi páribe.
What do they call this in Uriya?	ଓଡ଼ିଆରେ ତାକୁ କଣ ବୋଲୁଛନ୍ତି ?	O'ḍiyáre táku koṇo bólutshonti?

ENGLISH.	URIYA.	ROMAN.
If I make any mistakes in speaking, correct me.	ଅମେ କଥାରେ କ ହେଲେ ହୁଡ଼ିଲେ ତୁମେ ଶୁଦ୍ଧ କରିବ ।	A′me kotháre ki hele huḍile tume s′uddho koribo.
You must read what you read last night over again.	ତୁ ଯୋଠାରେ କାଲି ରାତିରେ ପଢ଼ିଥିଲୁ କି ସେଠାରେ ଫେରେ ପଢ଼ିବାର ଅଛି ।	Tu jóṭháre káḷi rátire poḍhithiluki séṭháre phére poḍhibáro ochhi.
That word is not used here.	ଏ ଦେଶରେ ସେ କଥା ଚଳୁ ନାହିଁ ।	E dés′ore se kothá tsolu· náhiñ.
Is there any school in this village?	ଏ ଗାଁରେ ଚାଟଶାଳ ଅଛିକି ।	E gáñre tsáṭo-s′áḷo ochhiki?
The children read well, but their writing is not particularly good.	ପିଲାମାନେ ଭଲ କରି ପଢୁଛନ୍ତି ମାତ୍ର ତାଙ୍କର ଲେଖା ତେତେ ଭଲ ନାହିଁ ।	Pilámáne bholo-kori poḍhutshonti mátro táṇgkoro lekhá tete bholo náhiñ.
You have made a great many mistakes in spelling.	ତୁ ଅକ୍ଷରମାନେ ବନିବାରେ ବହୁତ ହୁଡ଼ କଲୁ ।	Tu okhyorománe bonibáre bohuto húḍo kolu.
Having never learnt anything, he is an utter fool.	ସେ କିଛି ପାଠ ନ କରିବା ହେତୁରୁ ସେ ଶୁଦ୍ଧ ମୂର୍ଖ ହୋଇଗଲା ।	Se kichhi páṭho no koribá héturu se s′uddho múrkho hoi-golá.

Why was the boy punished?	ସେ ପିଲାକୁ କାହିଁକି ଶିକ୍ଷା ହେଲା ।	Se piláku káhiñki s'ikhyá helá?
He was punished for being idle.	ସେ ଅଳସୁଆ ହେବା ହେତୁରୁ ତାକୁ ଶିକ୍ଷା ହେଲା ।	Se olos'uá hebá heturu táku s'ikhyá helá.
This book is torn; if you give it to the tailor, he will stitch it for you.	ଏ ପୁସ୍ତକ ଚିରିହୋଇଗଲା ଦର୍ଜୀକି ଦେଲେ ସିଲାଇ କରି ଦେବ ।	E pustoko chiri-hói-golá, dorjíki dele silái kori debo.
When I counted, there were thirty sheep.	ଆମ୍ଭେ ଗଣିଲା ବେଳେ ତିରିଶିଟା ମେଣ୍ଢା ଥିଲା ।	A'me gonilá bele tiris'itá menḍhá thilá.
In writing your accounts, do not use Uriya figures.	ତୋର ଲେଖା ଲେଖିବାର ଓଡ଼ିଆ ଅଙ୍କ ଲେଖ ନା ।	Tóro lekhá lekhibáro óḍiyá onko lekho ná.
If 4 nowties of grain sell for a Rupee, how many nowties will you get for fifty Rupees 12 annas; work that out quickly and tell me.	ଟଙ୍କାକୁ ଚାରି ନଉତି ଧାନ ହେଲେ ପଚାଶ ଟଙ୍କା ବାର ଅଣାକୁ କେତେ ହେବ ତାହା ଲେଖାକରି ବେଗେ କହ ।	Ṭonkáku tsári nouti dháno hele potsás'o ṭonká báro oṇáku kete hebo, táha lekhá-kori bege koho.

ON RIDING.

V.

ON RIDING.	ଘୋଡ଼ା ଚଢ଼ି ବୁଲିବାବିଷୟ ।	GHO'-ḌÁ TSOḌHI BALIBÁ BISHOYO.
ENGLISH.	URIYA.	ROMAN.
He rides every day.	ସେ ନିତି ଘୋଡ଼ା ଚଢ଼ୁଛି ।	Se niti ghóḍá tsoḍhuchhi.
The stirrup-leather broke, and he fell from his horse.	ରିକାବ ଚର୍ମ ଛିଡ଼ିଯିବାରୁ ସେ ଘୋଡ଼ା ଉପରୁ ପଡ଼ିଗଲା ।	Rikábo tsormo chhiḍi-jibáru se ghóḍá uporu poḍi-golá.
Has the horse-keeper not boiled the horse's gram yet?	ଘୋଡ଼ାସାଣୀ ଆଉରି କୋଳଥ ସିଝି ନାହିଁକି ?	Ghóḍásáṇí áuri kóḷotho sidzi náhiñki ?
No: he has neither wood nor pot for boiling it in.	ନାହିଁ ତାହା ସିଝାଇବା ପାଁରେ କାଠ ନାହିଁ ହାଣ୍ଡି ନାହିଁ ।	Náhiñ, táhá sidzáibá páñre káṭho náhiñ, háṇḍi náhiñ.
Gram is very cheap now, how many nowties do you get for a Rupee?	କୋଳଥ ଏବେ ବଡ଼ ସସ୍ତା ଟଙ୍କାକୁ କେତେ ନଉଛ ?	Kóḷotho ebe boḍo sostá, ṭonkáku kete nouti ?

Bring 3 bundles of straw for my horse.	ଆମର ଘୋଡ଼ା ପାଇଁ ତିନିଟା ବିଡ଼ା ଛଣ ଆଣେ ।	A'moro ghóḍá páiñ tiniṭá biḍá tshoṇo áne.
The horse was very dirty when I saw it this morning.	ଆଜି ସକାଳେ ଘୋଡ଼ାକୁ ଦେଖିଲା ବେଳକୁ ସେ ବଡ଼ ମହଳିଆ ହୋଇଥିଲା ।	A'ji sokáḷe ghóḍáku dekhilá beḷoku se boḍo mohoḷiá hóithilá.
That horse's tail wants cutting.	ସେ ଘୋଡ଼ାର ଲାଞ୍ଜ କାଟିବାର ଲୋଡ଼ା ।	Se ghóḍáro lándzo káṭibáro lóḍá.
Clean the horse first, and give him his corn afterwards.	ଘୋଡ଼ାକୁ ଆଗରେ ନିର୍ମଳ କରି କରି ସେଥି ଉତ୍ତାରୁ ତାକୁ ଦାନା ଦେ ।	Ghóḍáku ágore nirmoḷo kori kori sethi uttáru táku dáná de.
The horse appears to me to be lame.	ସେ ଘୋଡ଼ା ଛୋଟା ହୋଇଥିଲାପରି ମୋତେ ଦିଶୁଛି ।	Se ghóḍá tshóṭá hóithilá-pori móte dis'uchhi.
Tell the horse-keeper to saddle the horse and bring him round.	ଘୋଡ଼ାକୁ ଜୀନ ବାନ୍ଧିକରି ଆଣିବାର ଅଛି ବୋଲି ଘୋଡ଼ାସାଣୀକି କହ ।	Ghóḍáku jíno bándhi-kori áṇibáro ochhi bóli ghóḍásáṇíki koho.
Bring the horse's bridle.	ଏ ଘୋଡ଼ାର ବାଗ ଆଣେ ।	E ghóḍáro bágo áṇe.
Take the horse to the stable.	ଘୋଡ଼ା ଶାଳକୁ ନେଇଯା ।	Ghóḍá s'áloku néi-já.

English.	Uriya.	Roman.
Can my horse swim this river?	ଆମର ଘୋଡ଼ା ଏ ନଦୀ ପହଁରି ପାରୁଛିକି ?	A'moro ghóḍá é nodí pohoñri páruchhiki?
Take care that he does not get drowned.	ସେ ନ ବୁଡିଗଲା ପରି ଜାଗ୍ରତ କର ।	Se no buḍi-golá pori dzágroto koro.
Can a horse get to the top of that mountain?	ସେ ପର୍ବତ ଉପରକୁ ଘୋଡ଼ା ଚଢ଼ି ପାରିବକି ?	Se porboto uporoku ghóḍá tsoḍhi páriboki?
Can grass for the horse be procured there?	ଘୋଡ଼ା ପାଇଁ ସେଠାରେ ଘାଁସ ମିଳିବକି ?	Ghóḍá páiñ séṭháre gháñso miliboki?
It costs 20 Rupees a month to keep a horse.	ଘୋଡ଼ାକୁ ରଖିବା ପାଇଁ ମାସକୁ କୋଡ଼ିଏ ଟଙ୍କା ଲାଗିବ ।	Ghóḍáku rokhibá páiñ másoku kóḍie ṭonká lágibo.
This horse must be shod to-morrow morning early.	ଏ ଘୋଡ଼ାକୁ କାଲିକି ଲାଲ ବନ୍ଧାଇବାର ଅଛି ।	E ghóḍáku káliki lálo bondháibáro ochhi.
That bundle of grass is not enough for one horse.	ସେ ଘାଁସ ବିଡ଼ାକ ଗୋଟିଏ ଘୋଡ଼ାକୁ ଅଣ୍ଟିବ ନାହିଁ ।	Se gháñso biḍáko gótie ghóḍáku onṭibo náhiñ.

ON SHOOTING.

VI.

ON SHOOTING.	ବେଣ୍ଟ ବିଷୟ ।	BEṆṬO BISHOYO.
ENGLISH.	URIYA.	ROMAN.
I shall go out shooting early to-morrow morning.	କାଲି ବଡ଼ ସକାଳେ ବେଣ୍ଟକୁ ଯିବା ।	Káli boḍo sokáḷe benṭoku jibá.
Call me at cock-crow.	କୁକ୍କୁଡ଼ା ଡାକିବାବେଳେ ଆମକୁ ଡାକିଦେ ।	Kukkuḍá ḍákibá beḷe ámoku ḍáki-de.
Awake me before it is light.	ଉଜ୍ଜ୍ୱଳ ନ ହୋଉଣୁ ଆମକୁ ଉଠା ।	Udzdzwolo no hóuṇu ámoku uṭhá.
What animals are there in this jungle?	ଏ ବଣରେ କି କି ଜନ୍ତୁ ଅଛି ।	E boṇore ki ki dzontu ochhi?
There are sambur, spotted deer, wild boar, barking deer and hares.	ସମ୍ବର, ଯ୍ୟାଦ, ବାରହା, କୁଟୁରା, ଖୁଦୁର ଏ ସବୁ ଅଛି ।	Somboro, jyádo, bárihá, kuṭuṛá khuduro e sobu ochhi.

English	Uriya.	Roman.
There are also pea-fowl.	ମୟୂର ମଧ୍ୟ ଅଛି ।	Moyuro modhyo ochhi.
Have you got powder, shot and everything else ?	ତୁମ୍ଭଠାରେ ଦାରୁ ଗୁଳି ଏ ସବୁ ଅଛିକି ?	Tumbhoṭháre dáru guli e sobu ochhiki ?
A cheeta killed one of my lambs last night.	କାଲି ରାତ୍ରି ବାଘ ଗୋଟିଏ ମୋର ମେଣ୍ଢା ପିଲାକୁ ଗୋଟିଏ ମାରିପକାଇଲା ।	Káli rátri bágho g'oṭie móro menḍhá piláku góṭie mári pokáilá.
If I shoot the cheeta, I will make you a present of 5 Rupees.	ସେ କରଡ଼ାପତ୍ରିଆ ବାଘକୁ ଲାଛିଲେ ତୋତେ ପାଞ୍ଚ ଟଙ୍କା ଇନାମ ଦେବୁ ।	Se koroḍápotriyá-bághoku láchhile tóte pántso ṭonká inámo debu.
Who fired ?	କେସେ ଲାଛିଲା ?	Kése láchhilá ?
A paik fired, but the bullet missed.	ଗୋଟିଏ ପାଇକ ଲାଛିଲାନି, ଗୁଳି ଫିଟିଗଲା ।	Góṭ e páiko láchhiláni guḷi phiṭi-golá.
Do you think that I hit him ?	ଗୁଳି ବାଜିଲାପରି ତୋତେ ଦିଶିଲାକି ?	Guḷi bájilá pori tóte dis'iláki ?
Yes, the animal is wounded.	ହଁ ଜନ୍ତୁ ଘାଉଆ ହୋଇଅଛି ।	Hoñ, dzontu gháuá hói-ochhi.
My gun missed fire.	ମୋର ନଳି ଫୁଟିଲା ନାହିଁ ।	Móro noḷi phuṭilá náhiñ.
Are there any bears in that hill ?	ସେ ଡିମିରାରେ ଭାଲୁ ଅଛି କି ?	Se ḍimiráre bhálú ochhiki ?

There are, but nothing will break, as the caves are large and numerous.	ଭାଲୁ ଅଛି ମାତ୍ର ଦଲିମାନେ ବଡ଼ ହେବାରୁ କିଛି ବାହାରିବ ନାହିଁ ।	Bhálú ochhi mátro dolimáne boḍo hebáru kichhi báháribo náhiñ.
I saw tracks of bear on the other side of the mountain.	ପର୍ବତକୁ ସେ ଆଡ଼କୁ ଭାଲୁ ଗୋତ୍ରା ଦେଖିଲି ।	Porbotoku se áḍoku bhálú gotrá dekhili.
If you had beaten properly, plenty of game would have broken.	ତୁମେ ଭଲକରି କାଳିଥିଲେ ବହୁତ ଜନ୍ତୁ ବାହାରିଥାନ୍ତେ ।	Tume bholokori kálithile bohuto dzontu báhárithánte.
The bears come to eat the sugarcane at night time.	ଭାଲୁମାନେ ରାତ୍ରିରେ ଆଖୁ ଖାଇବାକୁ ଆସନ୍ତି ।	Bhálúmáne rátrıre ákhu khái-báku ásonti.
We must wait here.	ଆମ୍ଭେମାନେ ଏଠାରେ ଜଗିବାର ଅଛି ।	A'mbhemáne eṭháre dzogibáro ochhi.
Look ! there's a jackal.	ହେଟି ବିଲୁଆ ଅଛି ।	Héṭi biluá ochhi.
Slip the dog.	କୁକ୍କୁରକୁ ଛାଡ଼ିଦେ ।	Kukkuroku tsháḍi-de.
That dog is not at all well, he has worms.	ସେ କୁକ୍କୁର ଦେହରେ ସୁଖ କିଛି ନାହିଁ ତାର ପେଟରେ ପୋକ ଅଛି ।	Se kukkuro déhore sukho ki-chhi náhiñ táro peṭore poko ochhi.

ENGLISH.	URIYA.	ROMAN.
Are there any ducks in that tank?	ସେ ବନ୍ଧରେ ହଂସ ଅଛିକି ?	Se bondhore hoñgso ochhiki?
Have you seen any antelope?	ହରିଣ ଦେଖିଲୁକି ?	Horiṇo dekhiluki?
There are not many bison or nilgái in this part of the country.	ଦେଶର ଏ ଭାଗରେ ଗୟେଳ ଅବା ଘୋଡ଼ାଙ୍ଗ ବହୁତ ନାହାନ୍ତି ।	Dés'oro é bhágore goyeḷo obá ghóḍángo bohuto náhánti.
What bird is that?	ସେ କି ପକ୍ଷି ?	Se ki pokhi?
It is a vulture.	ସେ ସାର୍ଗୁଣା ପକ୍ଷି ।	Se sárguṇá pokhi.
Its wing is broken, it cannot fly.	ତାର ଡେଣା ଭାଗିଯାଇଥିବା ହେତୁରୁ ସେ ଉଡି ନ ପାରଇ ।	Táro ḍeṇá bhági-jáithibá héturú se uḍi no pároi.
Melt this lead in the fire and cast some bullets.	ଏ ସୀସାକୁ ନିଆରେ ତରଳାଇ ଗୁଳି ତୟାର କରେ ।	E' sísaku niáre toroḷái guḷi toyáro kore.

ON TRAVELLING.

VII.

ON TRAVELLING.	ପ୍ରୟାଣ ବିଷୟ ।	PROYA'ṆO BI'SHOYO.
ENGLISH.	URIYA.	ROMAN.
How much farther is it?	ଆଉର କେତେ ଦୂର ଅଛି ?	A'uri kete dúro ochhi?
How far is it from here to that village?	ଏଠାକୁ ସେ ଗାଁକୁ କେତେ ଦୂର ଅଛି ?	Eṭháku se gáñku kete dúro ochhi?
It is about $2\frac{3}{4}$ kós.	ରମାରମୀ ଦୁଇ କୋଶ ତିନ ପା ହେବ ।	Romạromí dui kós'o tini pá hebo.
I have nothing to eat.	ମୋତେ ଖାଇବାକୁ କିଛି ନାହିଁ ।	Móte kháibáku kichhi náhiñ.
I am hungry and thirsty.	ମୋତେ ଭୋକ ଶୋଷ କରୁଛି ।	Móte bhóko s'ós'o koruchhi.
Shew me the road to the village.	ଗାଁକୁ ଆମକୁ ବାଟ ଦେଖା ।	Gáñku ámoku báṭo dekhá.

ENGLISH.	URIYA.	ROMAN.
I want 3 carts, go and feteh them at once.	ଆମକୁ ତିନିଟା ଶଗଡ଼ ଲୋଡ଼ା ଅଛି ତକ୍ଷଣରେ ଘେନିଆଣେ ।	A'moku tinitá s'ogodo lóḍa ochhi, tokhyoṇore gheni-áṇe.
The wheel of the cart came off.	ଶଗଡ଼ର ଗୁଲି ବାହାର ପଡ଼ିଲା ।	S'ogoḍoro guḷi báhári poḍilá.
The bullocks can walk no farther.	ବଳଦମାନେ ଆଉ ଚାଲି ପାରୁନାହାନ୍ତି ।	Boḷodománe áu tsáḷi páru-ná-hánti.
Send that cart away.	ସେ ଶଗଡ଼ ପଠାଇଦେ ।	Se s'ogoḍo poṭhái-de.
Pay the cartman his hire, and let him go.	ଶଗଡ଼ିଆକୁ ଭଡ଼ା ଦେଇପକା ସେ ଯାଉ ।	S'ogoḍiáku bhoḍá deí-poká, se jáu.
Hulloh! you bandy man, move your cart out of the way.	ଅରେ ଶଗଡ଼ିଆ ବାଟରୁ ଶଗଡ଼ କାଢ଼ିଦେ ।	A're s'ogoḍiá, bátoru s'ogoḍo káḍhi-de.
Can't you hear?	ତୋର କାନକୁ ଶୁଭୁ ନାହିଁକି ?	Tórokánoku s'ubhu náhiñ-ki?
When I called to you, why did you not move your cart out of the way?	ମୁ ଡ଼ାକିଲା ବେଳେ ତୁ ବାଟରୁ ଶଗଡ଼ କାହିଁକି କାଢ଼ୁ ନାହୁଁ ।	Muñ ḍákilá beḷe tu báṭoru s'ogodo káhiñ-ki káḍhu na-huñ.

I want 2 coolies to carry my things.	ଆମର ସାମାନ ବୋହିନେବାକୁ ଦୁଇ ଜଣ ମୁଲିଆ ଲୋଡ଼ା ।	A'moro sámáno boninebáku dui dzoṇo muliá lóḍá
What are the coolies doing?	ମୁଲିଆମାନେ କଣ କରୁଛନ୍ତି ।	Muliámáné kono korutshonti?
They are cooking their rice.	ସେମାନେ ଭାତ ରାନ୍ଧୁଛନ୍ତି ।	Semáne bháto rándhutshonti.
What! have they not eaten yet?	କଣ ଅଉରି ଖାଇନାହାନ୍ତିକି ?	Koṇo áuri khái náhánti ki?
How much is each cooly to get?	ଗୋଟିଏ ମୁଲିଆକୁ କେତେ ଲେଖାରେ ଦେବାର ଅଛି ।	Góṭie muliáku kete lekháre debáro ochhi.
Give each man 4 annas.	ତାଙ୍କୁ ଜଣକୁ ଶୁକାଏ ଲେଖାରେ ଦେ ।	Tángku dzoṇoku s'úkáe lekháre de.
I have lost my way, show me the road.	ମୁଁ ବାଟ ବଣା ହୋଇ ଗଲି ମୋତେ ବାଟ ଦେଖା ।	Mu báṭo boṇá hói-goli, móte báṭo dekhá.
Bring a lighted torch.	ଦୁହୁଡ଼ି ଲଗାଇ କରି ଆଣ ।	Duhuḍi logái-kori áṇo.
Call the kárji of the village.	ଗାଁ କାର୍ଯିକି ଡାକି ଦେ ।	Gáñ kárjí-ki ḍáki de.
You must get me some sheep, goats, chickens, milk and eggs.	ଅମ୍ଭ ପାଇଁ ମେଣ୍ଢା ଛେଳି କୁକୁଡ଼ା ଦୁଧ ଆଉ ଡିମ୍ବ ସରପରା କରିବାର ଅଛି ।	A'mbho páiñ menḍhá, chheḷi, kukkuḍá, dudho áu ḍimbo soroporá koribáro ochhi.

English.	Uriya.	Roman
What things have you for sale?	ତୋଠାରେ ବିକିବାକୁ କି ଶରକ ଅଛି ।	Tóṭháre bikibáku ki s′oroko ochhi.
Go to the bazar, and buy some rice, sugar, salt and oil.	ବଜାରକୁ ଯାଇ ଚାଉଳ ନବାତ ନୁଣ ଆଉରି ତେଲ କିଣିଆଣେ ।	Bodzároku jái tsáuḷo nobáto nuṇo áuri telo kiṇi-áṇe.
These things are not at all cheap, they are very dear.	ଏ ଚିଜ କିଛି ସସ୍ତା ନାହିଁ ବଡ଼ ମହର୍ଗ ହୋଇ ଅଛି ।	E chidzo kichhi sostá náhiñ, boḍo mohorgo hói ochhi.
This thing is old, and I will not buy it.	ଏ ଶରକ ପୁରୁଣା ହେବାରୁ ଆମେ କିଣିବୁ ନାହିଁ ।	E s′oroko puruṇá hebáru áme kiṇibu náhiñ.
Never mind; I don't want it.	କିଛି ଚିନ୍ତା ନାହିଁ, ଆମକୁ ଲୋଡ଼ା ନାହିଁ ।	Kichhi chintá náhiñ, ámoku lóḍá náhiñ.
What is the price of that sheep?	ସେ ମେଣ୍ଢା କେତେ ?	Se meṇḍhá keṭe?
Two rupees.	ଦୁଇ ଟଙ୍କା ।	Dui ṭonká.
Bring a Kávadi-man to carry the things.	ମୋର ସରଞ୍ଜାମ ବୋହିନେବାକୁ ଗୋଟିଏ ଭାରୁଆ ଆଣେ ।	Móro sorondzámo bóhi-nebá-ku góṭie bháruá áṇe.

Pitch the tent under a tree near the tank.	ତମ୍ବୁ ବନ୍ଧ ତଡ଼ ଗଛ ତଳେ ମାରିବାର ଅଛି ।	Tombu bondho todo gotsho tole máríbáro ochhi.
That rope is slack, pull it tant.	ସେ ଦୌଡ଼ି ହୁଗୁଳା ହୋଇଅଛି ତାକୁ ଭିଡ଼ିକରି ବାନ୍ଧେ ।	Se douḍi hugulá hói-ochhi táku bhiḍi-kori bándhe.
Two of the tent ropes are missing and the tent pegs have also all been lost.	ତମ୍ବୁ ଦୌଡ଼ି ଦୁଇଟା ହଜିଗଲା ମେଖ ମଧ୍ୟ ସବୁ ହଜିଗଲା ।	Tombu douḍi duiṭá hoji-golá mekho modhyo sobu hoji golá.
Strike the tent, after I have left.	ଆମେ ବାହାରିଗଲା ଉତ୍ତାରୁ ତମ୍ବୁ କାଢ଼ି ଦଅ ।	A'me báhári-golá uttáru tombu káḍhi-dio.
Take my tent down to-night, and take it on to Aska. I shall be there to-morrow morning, and shall stay there for three days.	ଆଜି ରାତିରେ ଆମର ତମ୍ବୁ କାଢ଼ିକରି ଆସିକାକୁ ନିଅ, କାଲି ସକାଳେ ସେଠାକୁ ଆସିବା । ଆସିକରି ତିନ ଦିନ ରହିବା ।	A'ji rátire ámoro tombu káḍhi-kori ásikáku nio, káli sokáḷe seṭháku ásibu, ásikori tini dino rohibá.
I want some cold water for bathing.	ସ୍ନାନ କରିବା ପାଇଁରେ ଆମକୁ କାକର ପାଣି ଲୋଡ଼ା ଅଛି ।	Snáno koribá páñre ámoku kákoro páṇi lódá ochhi.

ENGLISH.	URIYA.	ROMAN.
Bring some hot water.	ତତଲା ପାଣି ଆଣିଦେ ।	Totolá páṇi áṇi-de.
How much water is there in the river?	ନଦୀରେ କେତେ ପାଣି ଅଛି ?	Nodíre kete páṇi ochhi?
Is the water deep here?	ଏଠାରେ ପାଣି ଗମ୍ଭୀର ଅଛିକି ?	Eṭháre páṇi gobhíro ochhi ki?
Is the tide in the river?	ଏବେ ନଦୀରେ ଜୁଆର ଦେଇଛିକି ?	Ebe nodíre dzuáro déichhi-ki?
The tide is not in yet.	ଆଉରି ଜୁଆର ଦେଇନାହିଁ ।	A'uri dzuáro déi-náhiñ.
Is there a bridge over the river?	ନଦୀ ଉପରେ ସଙ୍ଖ ଅଛିକି ?	Nodí upore sonkho ochhi ki?
Hullo! boatman how am I to cross this river?	ଅରେ ନାଉଡ଼ିଆ ଏ ନଦୀରେ ଅମ୍ଭେ କିପରି ଯିବା ?	A're náuḍiá é nodíre ámbhe kipori jibá?
This bridge is old, and requires repair.	ଏ ସଙ୍ଖ ପୁରୁଣା ହୋଇଗଲା ତାକୁ ମରାମତ କରିବାର ଅଛି ।	E sonkho puruṇá hói-golá táku morámoto koribáro ochhi.
Where can I cross the river?	ଏ ନଦୀ କୋଠାରେ ପାରି ହେବୁ ?	E' nodí kóṭháre pári hebu?
Clean the boat out, and bring it.	ନାଆ ନିର୍ମଳ କରି କରି ଆଣେ ।	Náá nirmoḷo kori kori áṇe.

Hoist the sail.	ଅଦ୍ଝାଲତ ବାନ୍ଧେ ।	Odzháloto bándhe.
There is no wind.	ପବନ କିଛି ନାହିଁ ।	Pobono kichhi náhiñ.
Take down the sail.	ଅଦ୍ଝାଲତ କାଢ଼ିଦେ ।	Odzháloto káḍhi-de.
Can't you feel the bottom with your pole ?	କି କାତବାଡ଼ି ପାଉ ନାହିଁକି ?	Ki káto-báḍi páu náhiñ-ki ?
Anchor the boat here.	ନାଆକୁ ଏଠାରେ ନଙ୍ଗଳିଦେ ।	Nááku éṭháre nongoḷi-de.

MISCELLANEOUS.

VIII.

MISCELLANEOUS.	ବିଶେଷ କଥାବାର୍ତ୍ତା ।	BI'SE'SHO KOTHA'BA'RTTA'.
ENGLISH.	URIYA.	ROMAN.
Pull the punka.	ପଂଖା ଝିକେ ।	Ponkhá jhike.
It is very hot to-day.	ଆଜି ବହୁତ ଗରମ ହୋଇଅଛି ।	A'ji bohuto goromo hói-ochhi.
It looks like a storm.	ବତାସ ପବନ ଆସିବାପରି ଦିଶୁଛି ।	Botáso pobono ásibạ́-pori dis'uchhi.
It is very dark just now.	ଏବେ ବଡ଼ ଅନ୍ଧାର ହୋଇଅଛି ।	Ebe boḍo ondháro hói-ochhi.
The wind is rising.	ପବନ ଅଣ୍ଟ ହୋଇ ଆସୁଅଛି ।	Pobono áṇto hói ásuchhi.
The wind is blowing hard.	ପବନ ବହୁତ ବହୁଛି ।	Pobono bohuto bohuchhi.
The branch of that tree has been broken off by the wind.	ସେ ଗଛର ଡାଳ ପବନରେ ଭାଗିଗଲା ।	Se gotshoro ḍálo pobonore bhági-golá.
The lightning flashes.	ବିଜୁଳି ମାରୁଛି ।	Bidzuḷí máruchhi.

It is thundering.	ଗର୍ଜନ କରୁଛି ।	Gordzono koruchhi.
It is very cloudy and looks like rain.	ବହୁତ ମେଘ କରୁଛି ବର୍ଷିବାପରି ଦିଶୁଛି ।	Bohuto mégho koruchhi borshibá-pori disuchhi.
Bring me my umbrella.	ଅମର ଛତା ଆଣେ ।	A'moro tshotá áṇe.
The rain has ceased.	ବର୍ଷା ଛାଡ଼ିଗଲା ।	Borshá tshádi-gola.
The sun is very powerful now. I am tired, let us sit down in the shade and rest a bit.	ଏବେ ବଡ଼ ଖରା କାଟୁଛି ହାଲିଆ ହେଲୁ ଗଛ ଛାଇରେ ବସିକରି ଟିକିଏ ହାଲିଆ ମାରିବା ।	Ebe boḍo khorá káṭuchhi háliá helu gotsho tsháire bosikori ṭikie háliá máribá.
Two people were killed by lightning.	ବଜ୍ର ପଡ଼ିବାରୁ ଦୁଇ ଜଣ ମରିଗଲେ ।	Bodzro poḍibáru dúi dzoṇo mori-gole.
A great deal of dew falls in the cold weather.	ଶୀତ କାଳରେ ବହୁତ କାକର ପଡୁଛି ।	S'íto káḷore bohuto kákoro poḍuchhi.
My feet are very cold.	ମୋର ପାଦମାନେ ବଡ଼ କାକର ହୋଇଅଛି ।	Móro pádománe boḍo kákoro hói-ochhi.
Light a fire.	ନିଆ ଲଗା ।	Niá logá.

English	Uriya.	Roman.
If the house caught fire, it would soon burn down.	ଘରେ ନିଆ ଲାଗିଲେ ବେଗେ ଜଳିଯିବ ।	Ghore niá lágile bege dzoḷ jibo.
I sent for the carpenter, but he said that he would not come.	ମୁଁ ସେ ବଢ଼ାଇ ପାଇଁ ପଠାଇଲିନି ସେ ଆସିବ ନାହିଁ ବୋଇଲା ।	Muñ se boḍhai páiñ poṭháilini se ásibi nahiñ bóilá.
You must saw this beam in two.	ଏ କାଠୁଟା ତୁମେ କର୍ତ୍ତରେ ଚିରିଦେବାର ଅଛି ।	E káṭhuṭá tume kortore chir debáro ochhi.
Go and buy me three planks to make a door.	କବାଟ ତିଆର କରିବାକୁ ତିନିଟା ପଟା କିଣି ଆଣିଦେ ।	Kobáṭo toyáro koribáku tiniṭá poṭá kiṇi áṇi-de.
The roof of this house must be re-thatched.	ଏ ଘର ଚାଳ ନୂଆ ଛଣରେ ଛାଇବାର ଅଛି ।	E ghoro tsáḷo nuá tshoṇre tsháibáro ochhi.
If you tile your house it will not catch fire.	ତୋର ଘର ଝିଂକର କଲେ ନିଆଁ ଲାଗିବ ନାହିଁ	Tóro ghoro jhinkoro kole, niá lágibo nahiñ.
Why don't you knock down that mud wall and build a brick one instead?	ସେ ମାଟିକାନ୍ଥ ଭାଙ୍ଗିଦେଇ ତୁ କାହିଁକି ଇଟା କାନ୍ଥ କରୁନାହିଁ ?	Se máṭí-kántho bhángi-dei tu káhiñki iṭṭá kántho koru-nahiñ?

Turn the cart to the left hand side.	ଶଗଡ଼କୁ ଡେବରି ଆଡ଼େ ବୁଲାଇଦେ ।	S'ogodoku debiri áde bulái-de.
Take the road to the right hand-side, and go straight on.	ଖାଇବା ହାତ ଆଡ଼େ ସଳଖ କରି ନେ ।	Kháibá háto áde so'okho kori ne
My husband knotted two ropes together and bound me.	ମୋର ଗିରସ୍ତ ଦୁଇ ଦଉଡ଼ିରେ ଗଣ୍ଠି ପକାଇ ମୋତେ ବାନ୍ଧିଦେଲେ ।	Móro girosto dui doudire gonthi pokái móte bándhi-dele.
When he seized your cloth why did you not shout out ?	ତୋର ଲୁଗାକୁ ଧରିବା ବେଳେ ତୁ କାହିଁକି ହୁରି କଲୁ ନାହିଁ ।	Tóro lugáku dhoribá bele tu káhiñki huri kolu-náhiñ ?
Eleven persons in my village fell sick of cholera, and only two recovered.	ଆମର ଗାଁରେ ଏଗାର ଜଣ ମନୁଷ୍ୟ ଝାଡ଼ା-ବାନ୍ତିରେ କାଇଲା ହୋଇ ମାତ୍ର ଦୁଇ ଜଣ ମନୁଷ୍ୟ ଭଲ ହୋଇ ଗଲେ ।	A'moro gáñre égaro dzono monushyo dzháda-bántire káilá hói, mátro dui dzono monushyo bholo hoi-gole.

A PRACTICAL HAND BOOK OF URIYA.

PART III.

Uriya depositions in the Roman Character with English translation.

N B.—The learner is advised to study the following depositions as specimens of the living language of *the people.* With a single exception, they were all taken down by the writer himself, and contain the very words of the speakers themselves.

FIRST WITNESS.

English.

About 26 or 27 days ago I was sleeping in my field. I looked up and saw people tying the corn together, and removing it from the field. Náná Nároṇo was tying a bundle together. I ran and laid hold of him with the bundle from behind. Upon catching hold of him, I shouted out, "They are stealing my corn, run." I then got frightened, for I thought that the Dandasí man might perhaps stab me or beat me, and so I untied the rope round the bundle and bound him with it. A'nondo A'tsári and Tsondro Moni then arrived, and upon their coming I brought him close to the watch-hut. As I was standing holding him, Gonga Dáso came up and told me to let him go. I said: "He was taking away my corn, why should I let him go? I will report (the matter) to the authorities." He said to me: "We will (first) see how much of your corn he has taken." I said: "I am holding the thief, do you go and see." A'nondo A'tsari and Gongadáso, these two went to have a look at the field. Directly afterwards Govindo Náyoko came up with a

PROTHOMO SA'KHI' LEKHA'IBA' BA'NGMU'LO.

O'ḌIYA'.

A'dzoku sotáis'i ki oṭháis'i dino hebo muñ bilore rátro káḷore s'ói-thili. Muñ tsáhilá soriki dháno bándhi-kori biloru jáuts-honti. Náná Nároṇo bólibá ásámi dháno gots-há bándhuchhi. Muñ dhái-goli. Gots-há sángore táku pots-ho áḍe dhori pokáili. Dhori pokáikori huri koli: Móro dháno tsóro gheni nóuts-honti dhái poḍo, huri koli. Se káḷore móte bhoyo lágilá Dondási lóko bhusi-pokáibo mári-pokáibo bóli bhoyo helá. Se gotsháro douḍi phiṭái táku bándhi-pokáili. A'nondo A'tsári áilá. Tsondro Moṇi á-ila. Emáne ásibáru táku bhóñra pákhoku neli. Sethi uttáru muñ táku dhori ṭhiyá hóichhi e Gongádáso bólibá ásámi ásile. Bóile táku ts-háḍe, ts-háḍe. Muñ bóili dháno bóhi-nelá muñ táku káhiñki ts-háḍibi sorkáruku dzoṇá koribi bóili. Se bóilá: "Tóro kete dháno néichhi-ki bilo dekhibá." Muñ bóili: "Muñ tsóri dhori ṭhiyá hóichhi, tume jái dekho." A'nondo A'tsári Gongádáso dui dzoṇo bilo dekhibáku gole. Se káḷore Gobindo Náyoko bólibá ásámi bhusá-káṭi dhorikori ásilá. Bóilá: "Tóte ke bándhichhi, bóli pots-

dagger in his hand, and asked: "Who has tied you?" I told him that he (the thief) had been carrying off my corn, and that I had bound him. He said: "If you don't let him go, I will cut you down," and raised his dagger. Having a stick in my hand at the time I struck him with it. He started back, and I called out; Hulloh! he is stabbing me, run! He again raised his dagger to strike me. I again struck him with my stick. At this moment Tsondro Moni Behara and Ononto Atsári came up, and upon their exclaiming: "What is this, have you come to stab him in the night-time?" he ran away. As he was running away, Gongáhári Dáso saw him, and also Anondo Atsári.

Afterwards Gongádhoro Dáso arrived, and said: "Although there were so many of us about the field he came to stab you. Let the thief go." I said: "He has taken my corn away, and you saw that he came to stab me, why should I let him go?" He said to me: "Inform the Sirkár (of it) I will be responsible for the grain that you have lost (idiom.)" Whereupon he released Nárono Náik. That is the whole of the matter.

hárilá. Muñ bóili: "Móro dháno nelá je, muñ bandhichhi." "Ts-háḍi debuki háṇi-debi," bóli-kori káṭi uporoku ṭekilá. Se kálore móro hátore báḍi thibáru táku piṭi-deli. Se pots-hoku ghunchi-golá: Móte háṇi-pokáilá hé, dhái-poḍo hé, bóli muñ koli. Auri thore háñibi bóli káṭi ṭekilá. Muñ áuri thore báḍire piṭi-deli. E somoyore Tsondro Moni Behárá Ononto Atsári hádzoro hele: "Ye kiho háṇi pokáuts-hu rátro kálore," bólibáru se poḷáilá. Se poḷáibá somoyore Gongáhári Dáso dekhichhi. Anondo A'tsári se modhyo dekhichhi.

Sethi uttáru e Gongádhoro Dáso ásilá. Ḅóilá: "A'me ete lóko bilore tháu tháu háñi pokáuchhi e tsóroku phiṭái dio." Muñ bóili: "Móro dháno nelá ebe móte haṇi pokáuthilá dekhilo, áu muñ kópori ts-háḍi debi." Se bóilá: "'Tume sorkároku dzoṇá koro e báḍi boḍolámuku muñ eká púchi, bólibáru se tsóro Nároṇo Náyokoku phiṭái delá. Seṭháre songoti setiki.

———

SECOND WITNESS.

English.

About 27 or 28 days ago I was sleeping in the field about 10 or 11 o'clock. The complainant made a noise, and upon his calling out that they were carrying off his grain, I ran. Tsondro Moni Behorá ran. Ononto Atsárjyo ran. When we got there, three or four people were running off with bundles of corn, and upon our pursuing them, they threw them down and ran away. The complainant was holding this man Nárono Náyoko, and by his side there was a bundle of corn. It was after this that we went. He (complainant) brought him close to the watch-house, and whilst we were sitting there, Gongá Dáso came up and said: "What is all this about, let the thief go." Whereupon (lit. upon his saying so) the complainant said: "He has taken away my corn, and I shall not let him go." Gongá Dáso said: "Go and see how much of your corn has been stolen." The complainant said: "I am holding the thief and cannot go, do you go and look at the field." Upon his saying this, Gongá Dáso took me with him, and we went off to look at the field. As we were looking at the field, the complainant shouted out that they were cutting him to pieces, and upon his saying this, we ran. When we got to the spot this

DWITI'YO SA'ḲHI' LEKHA'IBA' BA'NGMU'LO.

O'ḌIYA'.

A'dzoku sotáis'i ki oṭháis'i dino hebo rátro dos'o ghoḍiki egáro ghoḍi hebo, muñ bilore s'ói-thili. Dábádáro huri kolá: Móro dháno bóhi-nelá dhái-áso, bólibáru muñ dháili. Tsondromoṇi Behorá dháilá. Ononto A'tsárjyo dháilá. Golá beḷoku tini tsári dzoṇo dháno gots-há dhori poḷáuts-honti. A'me dháibáru se pokái-dei poḷáilá. Ye Nároṇo Náyokoku dábádáro dhorichhi. Dháno gotshá táhá pákhoku dhorichhi. A'me sethi uttáru golu. Táku bhóñrá pákhoku gheni áṇilá. Ye kálore seṭháre bosi-ots-hu. Gongá Dáso ásilá, boilá: "E ki átsorono, tsóroku tsháḍi de" bólibáru, dábádáro bóilá: "Móro dháno bóhi-nelá, muṇ ts-háḍibi ná-hiñ." Gongá Dáso bóilá: "Tóro kete dháno tsóri jáichhi bilo dekhá" bólibáru dábádáro bóilá: "Muñ tsóroku dhorichhi muñ jibi náhiñ, tume jái bilo dekho," bólibáru Gongá Dáso móte dhori se biloku dekhibáku golu. E káḷore áme biloku deḳhutsu. Dábádáro huri kolá: "Móte háṇi-pokáilá," bólibáru áme dhái-ásilu. A'ilá beḷoku e Gobindo Náyoko káṭi dhori poḷáuchhi. Tsondro Moṇi Behorá, Ononto A'tsário. ámoku kohile: "A'me eṭháre no thile, ehi khyoṇe háṇi dei-thántá; áme tsáhilá, beḷoku eḍe busá-káti dhori poḷáuthilá dekhilu." Se káḷore e Gongádáso dábádároku bóilá: Tóro

man Govindo Náyoko ran away with a knife in his hand (lit. holding a knife). Tsondro Moni Behor and Ononto Atsário said to us: "If we had not been here, he would have cut him down in another instant (lit. in this instant)." When we saw him, he was running away with a thrust-knife as long as this (indicating its length on his arm). Gongá Dáso then said to the complainant: "If he had stabbed you, you would have lost your life, let this thief go." Whereupon the complainant said: "He has taken away a lot of my corn, and I won't let him go." Gongá Dáso said (to him): "Give information to the authorities (Sirkar) and let him go." The complainant however would not, and so Gongá Dáso untied the thief and let him go. This is all I know, I know nothing more, Sir.

THIRD WITNESS.

Some 27 or 28 days ago I was sleeping in my field at night. The man named A'rtotá A'tsário shouted out, that they were carrying off his corn, and called to us to run. Accordingly I ran. When I got there, they were running off with 3 or 4 bundles of corn. When Anonto A'tsário, A'nondo A'tsário and myself saw (them) they threw down the bundles and ran off.

práṇo jái thántá ebe háṇi-pokáithile, e tsóroku tsháḍi-de, bólibáru dábádáro bóilá: Móro kete dháno nelá, muñ tsháḍibi náhiṇ, bóilá. Gongá Dáso bóilá: Tu sorkáruku dzoṇá kore, yáku tsháḍi-de. Dábádáro náhiñ bólibáru Gongá Dáso tshoḍái tsóroku ghouḍi delá. Etiki eká, áu muñ kichhi dzáṇi náhiñ, Bábu.

TRUTI'YO SA'ḲHI' LEKHA'IBA' BA'NGMU'LO.

A'dzoku sotáis'i ki oṭháis'i dino hebo se rátro mó bilore muñ s'ói-thili. A'rtótá A'tsário bólibá ásámi huri kolá: "Móro dháno neuchhi, dhái-áso," bóli huri kolá. Se somoyore muñ dhái-ásili. Muñ dhái-ásilá beḷoku tiniṭá tsáriṭá dháno gotsháku ḍhorikori poḷáu-thile. A'nonto A'tsário, A'nondo A'tsário, áme, dekhibáru gotshá pokái-kori

English.

The complainant was holding Nárono Náyoko by force. Upon our approach, he dragged him off to the side of the watch-hut. At this time, the man named Gongá Dáso arrived, (and) said to the complainant: "What is all this about, let him go." Whereupon the complainant said: "I caught him, how can I let him go?" Gongá Dáso said: "Go and look at your field, and see how much of your corn has been stolen." The complainant said: "I am holding the thief; if I let go, the thief will run away; do you go and examine it." Anondo Atsário taking Gongá Dáso with him (then) went to the field. At this time the man named Govindo Náyoko arrived and said: "Who bound you?" The complainant said: "I laid hold of him for stealing my corn." Govindo Náyoko said: "If you do not let him go, I will cut you down" (idiom.) and raised his knife in the air, (lit. upwards). The complainant had a stick in his hand which he raised. The Dandási retreated but came at him again, and raised his knife. The complainant shouted out: "He is killing me, run," and again menaced him with his stick. All this time we were sitting near the watch-house. We stood up and said: "Hulloh! Govindo Náyoko, what's all this about? Have you come to murder a Brahmin in the night time? If we had not been here this very minute you would have

poḷáile. Nároṇo Náyokoku dábádáro dzobordosti kori dhori-thilá. A'me jibáku bhóñrá pákhoku bhiḍi áṇiḷá. E káḷore Gongá Dáso bólibá ásámi se ásilá. Dábádáro'ku kohilá: "E ki kothá, tsháḍi de," bólibáru se dábádáro: "Muñ dhorichhi táku, kimiti ts-háḍibi" bólibáru, Gongá Dáso kohilá: "Kete dháno tóro tsóri jáichhi, já, bilo dekhibá." Dábádáro bóilá: "Muñ tsóroku dhorichhi ts-háḍi dele tsóro poḷáibo, tume jáo, dekhi áso." Anondo A'tsário Gongá Dásoku dhori-kori biloku gole. Se káḷore Gobindo Náyoko bólibá ásámi se ásilá. Se bóilá: "Tóte ke dhóila?" Dábádáro bóilá: "Muñ dhóili, móro málo tsóri nelá, muñ dhóili." Gobindo Náyoko bóilá: "Ts-háḍi debu-ki háṇi debi," káṭi uporoku untsáilá. Dábádáro ṭhengá dhori thilá táku untsáilá. Dondási se potshoku báhári-golá. A'u thore dhái ásilá, káṭi untsáilá. Dábádáro huri kolá: "Háṇi pokáilá dhái-poḍo," huri-kori se dábádáro ṭhengá untsáilá. A'me se káḷore bhoñra pákhore bosi-thilu. A'me ṭhiá kori: "Kíré Gobindo Náyoko e ki kothá, tu rátro káḷore bráhmoṇoku háṇibáku ásuts-hu. A'me no thile, ehiṅge háṇi-pokáuts-hu," ethiki bólibáru se poḷáilá. Se káḷore Gongá Dáso A'nondo Atsário se ásile. Se ási-kori dábádároku kohile: "Tóro dhonoku dhono golá, tóro práṇo jai-thántá, bráhmoṇo no thile háṇi-pokái-diontá, táku tsháḍi de. Táku no ts-háḍile áme báhári-gole, ekutiá thile háṇi debo,

murdered him." Whereupon he ran away. Gongá Dáso and A'nondo A'tsário then came up, and the former said to the complainant: "You have lost your property, and might have lost your life. If you had not been a Brahmin, he would have killed you. Let him go. If you don't let him go, and we leave you here by yourself, he will kill you, for, although there were so many people about, he came to kill you: so now let him go." The complainant said: "He has taken my property, and all of you saw that the man came to kill me, how can I let him go?" Gongá Dáso said: "Inform the authorities. If you keep him, you will lose your life to no purpose, and so let him go." He (complainant) said: "I shall not let him go." Whereupon he (Gongá Dáso) released him, and drove him off. This is all I know.

FOURTH WITNESS.

About 27 or 28 days ago, I was sleeping in the field at night time. At this time about 11 o'clock, A'roto A'tsario gave a shout and said: "Run, they have stolen all the corn from my field." I got up and ran. As I was running, Anondo Atsário and Tsondro Moni Behorá were also running

ete lóko tháu tháu háṇibáku ásilá. Ebe táku tsháḍi-de." Dábádáro bóilá: "Móro málo nelá, tume somoste dekhuts-ho háṇibáku ásilá, muñ táku kimiti ts-háḍi debi." Gongá Dáso bóilá: "Tu Sorkároku dzoṇá kore. Táku rokhile hokonáke práṇo jibo, táku tsháḍi-de." Se bóilá: "Muñ ts-háḍibi náhiñ" bóḷibáru, tshoḍái kori ghouḍi delá. Ethiki eká, áu dzoṇá nahiñ."

TSOTU'RTHO SA'ḲHI' LEKHA'IBA' BA'NGMU'LO.

Sotáis'i ki oṭháis'i dino hebo muñ rátro káḷore bilore s'ói-thili. E somoyore rátro egáro ghoḍiṭháre A'roto A'tsário huri pokáilá: "Dhái poḍo móro dháno biloru sobu tsóro gheni-gole bólibáru muñ uṭhi dháili. Dháilá beḷosoriki A'nondo A'tsário Tsondro Moṇi Bchorá modhyo dháu-otshont.

English.

They (*i. e.*, the thieves) were going off with three or four bundles of corn. Upon seeing us, they threw them down and ran off, and we went up to Arotá Atsário. When we got to him, he was holding Nárono Náyoko by force along with a bundle of corn. He afterwards dragged him round to the side of the watch-hut. Gongá Dáso afterwards ran up and asked: "Hulloh! What have you got hold of him for?" "He has stolen all my corn, and so I seized him." He said: "Why, how much of your corn is gone? let us go and see." The complainant said: "I am holding the thief, how can I let him go, do you go and see." Accordingly Gongá Dáso taking A'nondo A'tsári with him went to look at the field. I and Tsondro Moni Behorá sat down at the side of the watch-hut. At this time Govindo Náyoko came up (and) said: "Hulloh! Nárono, who has caught you?" The complainant said: "He has stolen my corn, and so I seized him: "You bastard Brahmin" said he, "will you let him go, or shall I cut you down?" Whereupon he raised his knife. A'roto A'tsário had a stick in his hand at the time, and raised it. Upon his lifting it up, he sprang back. Upon his approaching a second time with his knife raised, A'roto A'tsário shouted out: "Hulloh,! run, he is murdering me." Then Tsondro Moni and I said to him: "What's this! Govindo Náyoko, have

O'ḌIYA'.

l'iniṭá ki tsáriṭá dháno gotshámáne dhori jáuthile. A'moku dekhibáru pokáidei poḷáile. E somoyore A'roto A'tsário pákhoku golu. Golá beḷosoriki Nároṇo Náyokoku dháno songotore dzobordosti-kori dhorichhi. Se káḷore táku dhori-kori bhoñrá pákhoku bhiḍi-áṇilá. Tohiñ uttáru Gongá Dáso dhái áilá: "Kihe káhin-ki dhorits-ho," bólibáru Gongá Dáso bóilá: "Móro dháno sorboswo tsóráibáru muñ dhorichhi." Se bóilá: "Káhiñ, tumbhoro kete dháno jáichhi dekhibá tsálo." Dábádáro bọilá: "Múṭo tsóroku dhorichhi kimiti ts-háḍi-kori jibi, tu jái dekhe bólibáru Gongá Dáso A'nondo A'tsárioku dhori-kori bilo dekhibáku gọlá. Se bhóñrá pákhore Tsondro Moṇi Behorá, muñ bosi-thilu." E káḷore Gobindo Náyoko ásilá. Bóilá: "Kíre Nároṇo tóte kiése dhorilá?" Dábádáro bóila: "Móro dháno tsórái-nebáru muñ dhorili. Bóilá: "Gihálipuo (com. gyálopo) Báhmoṇo ts-háḍibuná? háṇi debi" bóli káṭi uporoku ṭekilá. Se káḷore A'roto A'tsário báḍi dhori-thilá. Táku ṭeki-delá. Ṭeki-debáru pots-hoku ghunchi-golá. Phére áu thore ási káṭiki ṭekibá káḷore A'rotá At'sário: "Dhái-poḍo he! háṇi pokáilá," bóli huri kolá. Se káḷore Tsondro Moṇi Behorá muñ: "Kíre Gobindo Náyoko tu rátro káḷore ási-kori Bráhmoṇoku háṇuts-hu. Brohmá hotiyá koribuki?" bólibáru bhusákáṭi dhori báhári golá. Se káḷore Gongá Dáso dhái-áilá. Bóila: "Ki A'reto

you come to kill a Brahmin in the night-time? Would you commit Brahmin murder?" Whereupon he ran off with his knife. Gongá Dáso then came up and said: "What's this, A'roto A'tsário; although we were all of us about, he wanted to murder you; if we had not been here, he would have killed you. Your property has just been stolen, and you might have lost your life. If we leave the place he'll kill you. Let go this thief:" Upon which the complainant said: "I shall not let him go. I shall inform the authorities." Gongá Dáso said: "Go and inform them!" and untying the rope that A'roto A'tsari held, he drove Nárono Náyoko away. Sir, this is all I know.

DEPOSITION MADE BY A WITNESS.

On Sunday, the 19th instant, at eight o'clock at night, we were sitting between this constable's house and my own, wrapped up in our blankets. At that time this constable came. When he arrived he had no belt on. He had on his trousers and coat. I noticed something round his waist. Upon noticing it, I ran and laid hold of him. I called out to Obodono Lobi to run and bring me a wick. He procured a wick (light) and came. Upon his

O'ḌIYA'.

A'tsário áme somoste tháu tháu tóte ḥáṇi pokáuthilá, áme no thîle háṇi pokáithántá, tóro ebe dháno golá, práṇo jái-thantá, áme poḷáiḷe haṇi pokáibo, tu e tsóroku ts-háḍi-de bólibáru dábádáro bóilá: "Muñ ts-hádibi náhiñ, muñ sorkárore dzoṇá koribi." Gongá Dáso bóilá: "Tu dzoṇá kore," bólibáru Gongá Dáso A'rotá A'tsáriṭháru douḍi phiṭái Nárono Náyokoku ghouḍi delá. Bábu, muñ ethiki dzáṇichhi.

SA'ḲHI' LEKHA'IBA' BA'NGMU'LO.

Robibáro dino oṅísi tárikhore se dino áṭho ghoṇṭo rátri góṭe komoḷo ghoḍái-kori e sipái ghoroku móro ghoroku modhyore bosi-thilu. E sipái sete beḷo-somoyore ásilá. A'silá beḷore dábáli bándhi-náhiñ. Surái kóṭo táro dehore ochhi. Táro oṇṭá móṭe dis'ilá. Dis'ibáru muñ dhái-jái-kori dhorili. Obodono Lobiki góṭe boḷitá dhorikori dhái-áso' bóli ḍákili. Se bóḷitá dhorikori ásilá. A'sibáru Kórṭ ágore thibá rongo rumáḷo guḍáre nuá nuṇo e mudái

coming up, I found that the defendant had some new salt round his waist (lit. in) wrapped up in the red handkerchief before the Court. I afterwards searched the defendant's house. Upon searching it, (I found that) he (the defendant) had placed this blue bag in the corner with a log of wood on the top. I brought it out and examined it. There was new salt in the bag. When I arrested the defendant, he had just been relieved and was returning from guard. I kept the salt and this man in the Treasury building, and reported (the matter) to the Superintendent in the morning. The prisoner admitted ten times that the red handkerchief was his. He admitted it yesterday on the 20th instant. The prisoner admitted that the blue bag was his. Chinniá and the defendant both live in the same house (lit. to Chinniá and that defendant these two persons one house there is). After the salt was discovered in the house I never asked Chinniá anything (*i. e.*, about it). I am not on bad terms with the prisoner (lit. to me and to this prisoner no enmity there is not).

DEPOSITION MADE BY A COMPLAINANT.

Last Sunday at sunset, I was sitting in my verandah which overlooks the street. These two men,

oṇṭáre bándhi-kori ochhi. Se uttáru mudái ghoro tonkhili. Tonkhilá beḷoku góṭie kóṇore e nílo sánchiku káṭho ghoḍái-kori rokhi-thilá. Táku káḍhi gheni-áṇili. Se sánchire nuá nuṇo thilá. Muñ mudáiki dhorilá beḷoku se pårá bodlái-kori ásilá. E nuṇoku ásámiki "treasury" gháṭore rokhi-kori Superintendentuku sokáḷe riporṭo koli. E rongo rumáḷo-koidíro bóli-kori koidí dos'o thore oppi-ghenichhi. Káli kóḍie tárikhore oppi gheni-chhi. Se níliyá sánchi móro bóli koidí oppi-ghenilá. E Chiniáku e mudáiki dui dzoṇongku góṭie ghoro ochhi. Nuṇo ghore mililá uttáru se Chiniáku muñ kichhi pots-hári-náhiñ. Móte e koidíki kichhi hírshá náhiñ.

DA'BA'DA'RO LEKHA'IBA' BA'NGMU'LO.

Goto Robibáro dinore súrjyo udeyo beḷosoriki ámbhó dáṇḍopiṇḍáre muñ bosithili. E Chelámáyá

English.

Chelamáyá and Jongomo passed by (lit. went). As they passed, they made enquiries of me as to whether I had any pieces of cloth. I fetched a piece and showed it to them (lit. before them). It was agreed that they should supply me with fourteen jackets, and should return me the two and a half yards excess out of twenty-one yards (delivered), and that I should pay one anna and nine pice for each jacket. Chelamáyá took the piece of cloth and left. He agreed to deliver everything on the 26th instant. Jongamo Guráya who was with him at the time has told me that he left last night for Berhampore, taking his family with him. He has cheated me and run away. I beg that the authorities will punish him according to the regulations, and restore my property to me. He has gone off after giving back to me the pieces which he had cut up for eleven jackets, but the rest he has not given me. Dzongomo Guráya says that Chelamáyá has taken seven yards with him. He will prove that he himself has 14½ yards. Chelamáyá does tailor's work. The value of the seven yards of cloth would be seven 4-anna pieces, (*i. e.*, 1 Re. 12 ans.).

O'ḌIYA'.

Dzongomo Guráyá e dui dzoṇo gole. Jái-kori móte tháno lugá tolásile. Muñ áṇi tángko ágore dekháili. Dekhái kori mirdzái siiñbáku nirnoyo koli. Ekóis'i godzoku tsouḍo mirdzái áu báki dui godzo oḍhe koná dei pokáibáku, puṇi góṭié mirdzáiku oṇáe tini pois'a lekháre nirnoyo helá. Se tháno dhori e Chelámáyá báhári ásilá. Tshobís'i táríkhore sobu dei-pokáibo bóli nis'tsoyo kolá. Goto rátrore táro kuṭumbo dhori Brohmopuruku báhári golá bóli táhá sángore jái-thibá Dzongomo Guráyá móte kohilá. Móte dogá páiṭi kori poḷái-golá. Táku Sorkároghoro poddhotimánongko prokáre sikhyá kori móro málo diáibáro ochhi. Móte egáro góṭie mirdzáiki ṣe koná chirikori dei jái-ochhi áu báki tothimá móte dei náhiñ. Chelomáyá sátho godzo dhori golápori Dzongomo Guráyá kohuchhi. E Dzongomo Guráyáṭháre tshouḍo godzo oḍhe thilá pori se rudzu poḍuchhi. E Chelámáyá dorjí páiṭi koruchhi. E sátho godzo thánoro khorído sátho s'úká hebo.

DEPOSITION MADE BY A COMPLAINANT.

English.

On Friday morning at 9 o'clock Head Constable Chelomáyá brought a necklace to my shop to weigh. Upon his telling me to weigh the gold, and to let him know whether it was good or bad, I weighed the golden necklace. When I had weighed it, I told him that the weight was three tolas and one grain. The Head Constable then said: "I have got another piece of the same gold with me, look at this." I did so, and found that the specimen differed from the gold in the piece that the Head Constable had with him. I told him that he had received one rupee less gold than the weight (of gold) supplied by him, and told him to take it to another shop and enquire, and that I was ready to take it of him at the price which any other shopkeeper might settle. The other shopkeeper fixed the same price upon it that I had. I afterwards left for my house to take my meal. After eating, I returned to the bazar, and sat down in my shop. This man Rama Sámi, then came up and abused me in terms which will not bear repeating (lit. which will not come to the mouth). Upon his abusing me thus, I told him that it was not proper of him. Chelomáyá after taking his meal was returning to the cutcherry, and seizing him by the hand, he dragged him off. After going 10 yards, he

DA'BA'DA'RO LEKHA'IBA' BA'NGMU'ḶO.

O'ḌIYA'.

S'ukrobáro dino sokáḷe no ghonṭo somoyore Chelámáyá bólibá "Head Constable" nánukolu mó dokánoku tuḷibáku áṇilá. Se suná tuḷikori móte se bholo mondo songoti kohibáro ochhi bólibá héture muñ se súná máḷiki tuḷili. Tuḷikori tini toḷá upore podikái ochhi bóli kohili. Se suná sombhondoro motshá móṭháre ochhi se motsháku dekho, bóli "Head Constable" kohilá. Kohibáru se Head Constableṭháre thibá motshá sunáku se suná tsháḍilá. Tóro tuḷoku góṭie ṭonká uṇá ochhi bóli muñ kohili. Kohilá uttáru dwitíyo dokánoku jái-kori bujhái-ghenibáro ochhi se jeuñ prokáre kohiboki dzáṇo móro, bóli muñ kohili. Muñ jeuñ dorore bándhiliná se dokánodáro séhi rúpore eká doro bándhilá. Se uttáru móro ghoroku kháibáku muñ bálári goli. Kháilá uttáru muñ bodzáruku ásili. A'sikori muñ dokánore bosi-ochhi. E Rámo Swámi bólibá lóko ási-kori tundoku no ásibá bháshámáne gáli delá. Gáli debáru: "E tóte uchito náhiñ, bóli muñ bóili. Chelomáyá bhódzono kori kocheriki ásu-thiḷá. Se ási-kori hátore dhori kori jhinki-dhori báhári-golá. Dos'o godzo golá uttáru táro hátoru tshoḍái kori móte góṭie tsápoḍá márilá. Góṭie bidhá márilá.

ENGLISH.

broke away from him, and struck me a slap on the face. He (also) struck me a blow with his fist. Whilst the people were trying to separate us, a brother of his came running up, and gave me a couple of kicks.

STATEMENT MADE BY PRISONER.

About eight days ago Rájibo Dákuá, a child nine years old, son of a man named Nokiyá in my village, was outside in the street eating tamarinds and wearing on his neck a gold bead bracelet. It was then 9 o'oclock of day. I called to him to come to the jungle to eat honey. Upon his coming with me, I took the child to a nullah which is in the jungle (forming) the boundary between Belogumá and Mádhobopoli. As I intended to take the gold bead necklace that was on the child's neck and to kill him I threw the child into the nullah, and pressing with my knee upon his waist, I twisted the child's neck round with both my hands. Upon my twisting his neck in this manner, the child died immediately. After the child was dead, I broke off the gold bead necklace that was on his neck with eight single beads and the centre ornament. One of the beads dropped on the ground. I was unable to find it. Afterwards I cleared away the earth to a depth of one span with my hand, and buried the child in the

O'ḌIYA'.

Táro áu góṭie bhái dhái ási-kori lókománe tshoḍáu tshoḍáu móte dzóḍie góiṭhá márilá.

KOIDI' LEKHA'IBA' BA'NGMU'LO.

A'dzoku romáromí áṭho dino hebo ámbho grámo rohoṇi Nókiyá bólibá ás'amiro puo Rájíbo Ḍákuá bólibá no borsho boyoso hebá pilá bekore suná rosuṇiá máḷi logái dáṇḍore thái koyáñ kháuthilá. Diboso tsári ghoḍi beḷo hói-thilá. Mohu kháibá pañre boṇoku ásibáro ochhi bóli se Rájíbo Ḍákuáku muñ ḍákili. Mó sáthire se pilá ásibáru Belogumá Mádhobopoli sondhi boṇore thibá gótie náḷoṭháku se piláku muñ neli. Táro bekore thibá suná rosuṇiá máḷi néi táku práṇore mári-pokáibáku móte mono hebáru se piláku se náḷo bhitore toḷe pokái-dei móro áñṭhure se piláro oṇṭá máḍi-bosi móro dui hátore se piláro beko móḍi-deli. Sepori móḍi debáru se pilá tokhyoṇore eká mori-golá. Se pilá mori-golá uttáru táro bekore thibá suná rosuṇiá máḷi aṭhogóṭi rosuṇiá góṭie miná thibáro muñ chhiṇḍái neli. Se rosuṇiáru góṭie rosuniá toḷe seṭháre eká poḍi-golá. Móté dis'ilá náhiñ. Tohiñ uttáru se náḷore tháu bóli háte gobhírore móro hátore máṭí káḍhi se piláku se gátore póti-deli. Se-

hole leaving it in the ditch. From thence I went to my village. At the time I killed the child, the sun was right over my head. After I had returned to my village, Rájibo Dákuá's father Nokiyá saw me the evening of the same day. He questioned me about his son having gone with me as some child had told him. I said that I knew nothing about it. At the same moment I left the village of Belogumá and went off to my aunt's house in the village of Mádhobopoli. I went to sleep in my aunt's house. At the break of day a Constable came and arrested me. Upon his asking me the reason of my running away from my village, I told him that I had run away, as I had committed an offence. I went with the constable and shewed him the place where I had buried Rájibo Dákuá. Upon clearing away the sand from the spot, the corpse appeared. I had taken the necklace that was on Rájibo Dákuá's neck and placed it in the purse in my waist. I gave the necklace to the constable at the village of Belogumá. When I brought Rajibo Dákuá from the village, I took him into the jungle for the express purpose of killing him, and of taking the bead necklace that was on his neck. I have stated the whole of the above circumstances truthfully as they occurred, and no one taught me what I was to say.

The statement made by the prisoner was taken down in the Uriya language and read over to him.

ṭháru móro grámoku ásili. Se piláku muñ mári pokáibá somoyore mundo uporoku beḷo ásibá somoyo hói-thilá. Mó grámoku ásilá uttáru Rajíbo Ḍákuáro bápo Nókiyá móte se dino sondhiyá káḷore dekhilá. Móro puo tóro sáthire jáithilá pori se pilá kohilá bóli potshárilá. Móte dzoṇá náhiñ bóli muñ kohili sebe eká muñ Belogumá grámoru báhári ási Mádhobopoli grámoku móro piyusi ghoroku báhári goli. Móro piyusingko ghoro bhitore muñ s'ói-thili. Rátro páhántiyá somoyore "constable" ási móte dhori-pokáilá. Kó héturu tu gáñru poḷái ásilu bóli "constable" móte potsháribáru, muñ dósho korithili je poḷái ásili bóli kohili. Muñ "constable" sáthire jái Rájíbo Ḍákuáku póti-debá sthoḷo dekháili. Se sthoḷore bálí káḍhibáru s'obo mililá. Rájíbo Ḍákuáro bekore thibáro máḷi muñ néi móro oṇṭáre thibá gánjiáre rokhithili. Se máḷi Belogumá grámore muñ "constable" hátoku deli. Rájíbo Ḍákuáku muñ grámoru ḍáki nelá beḷore eká táku práṇore mári pokái táro bekore thibá rosuṇiá máḷi nebáku móte mono hói muñ táku boṇoku ḍáki neli. Upore lekháibá jábonto kothá soto kori tsolithibáro muñ kohilini móte kése hele sepori kohibáro ochhi bóli sikhái náhánti. Koidí kohibáro O'ḍiyá bhásháre lekhi poḍhibáku helá.

FIRST WITNESS.

English.

On Thursday at 2 o'clock I arrived at the fair from my village. At 4 o'clock I bought a cloth. The price for the cloth was 11 annas 9 pice (lit. three 4 anna pieces, less 3 pice). After the price had been fixed I asked him to give me the cloth. Defendant said: "First put down your money." When he had said this, I told him that I would give him a Rupee, and that he must give me the change out of it. So saying I gave him a rupee. I gave him a good rupee and he gave me back a 4-anna piece and 3 pice. He rang the rupee in the air three times after receiving it, and placed it in his waist. I (then) said: "Give me my cloth." He tore (the stuff in two) and gave me one half of it for the cloth. As he gave it to me, I said: "This is thin, keep it, and give me back my Rupee." Upon my saying this, the defendant told me to throw the cloth away. I said: "Take off an anna, and give it to me." The cloth-merchant said that he would do no such thing. I stood there for a short time. A man close to me said: "You have made him tear up his stuff, take your cloth and come away, what more do you want?" I afterwards came away. After leaving I looked at the shops, and walked along looking at them, until I came to a fish shop and

PROTHOMO SA'ḲHI' LEKHA'IBA' BA'NGMU'LO.

O'ḌIYA'.

Gurubáro dino dui ghoṇṭoku muñ gáñru háṭoku ásili. Tsári ghoṇṭoku muñ gámontsá kiṇili. Se gámontsá páe uṇá tini s'úká mulo helá. Mulo helá káḷore: "Gámontsá ámbhoku dio" bóili. Mudái, "A'ge dábu thuo," bóilá. Bóilá káḷore, "Ṭonká debi báhuḍi báki khortso dei póká" bóli muñ bóili. Bóilá káḷore muñ ṭonká deli. Muṇ bholo ṭonká deli. Se góṭie s'úki góṭie pois'á delá. Sete beḷe eká se ṭonká ṭini thoro bodzáilá. Semiti neikori oṇṭáre dhorilá. Muñ bóili móro gámontsá dio. Se chiri-kori móte góṭáe gámontsá poṭe dei pokáilá. Delá káḷore muñ bóiḷi: E gámontsá káilá hétchi, e gámontsá rokhi-kori ámbhoro ṭonká ámbhoku dei pokáo," bólibáru "Gamontsá se áḍe phobáḍi de," bóli se mudái bóilá. Muñ bóili: "Se uporo oṇáṭá hele káṭi-kori dio." Se ḍerá: "Debi náhiñ eká," bóilá. Seṭháre ṭikie chhiḍá heli. Pákhore thibá lóko bóilá: "Táro gámontsá chiri delu, dhori-kori áso, áu káhiñ-ki?" Sethi uttáru muñ báhári ásili. Báhári ásikori pos'orá dekhhili. Se pos'orámánongku dekhi dekhi ásuchhi. A'sikori muñ mátsho pos'orá pákhore chhiḍá hóichhi. Tsoitoṇo Suáiñ bólibá lóko mátsho páiñ jáichhi. Emonto somoyore se gámontsá debá lóko se pos'oráṭháku ási, áso bóli móte jhinki-áṇilá.

ENGLISH.

stood there. Tsoitono Suáin had come for fish. At this time the man who had sold (lit. given) me the cloth came up to the shop, and telling me to come pulled me along. I then said to him: "What are you pulling me for?" The defendant said: "Come along with me." I went (back) to the place, where the cloth shop was. After getting there, the weaver said: "You gave me this Rupee." "I never gave it, Sir," said I. "There is a mark on my rupee, I took it from my money-box" (lit. I was holding it).

I said to a constable: "There was a mark on the Rupee which I gave (him) look and see." The constable said: "What sort of a mark was there on your Rupee?" I said: "There was a mark of turmeric upon it (lit. upon my Rupee)." Upon saying this, the constable procured the good Rupee and examined it. When he had examined it, there was a mark of turmeric upon it. The constable said: "Come along to the station." We went to the station. The rupee which I had given was a good one. The weaver rang it three times, and (then) put it away. It was the defendant who produced the bad Rupee (lit. tin,) which is in court.

O'ḌIYA'.

Sete beḷe muñ bóili : "Móte káhiñki jhinkutshu?" Se mudái : Seṭháku áso, bóilá. Se gámontsá dokáno jeuñṭháre thilá seṭháku muñ goli. Golá uttáru se ḍerá bóilá : "E ṭonká móte delu." "Dei náhiñ bábu, bóli muñ bóili." Móro ṭonkáre chihno ochhi muñ koráṭore dhori-thili, bóli muñ kohili. Muñ constableku" bóili : "Muñ debá ṭonkáre chihno ochhi dekho," bólibáru se constable bóilá : "Tóro ṭonkáre ki chihno ochhi?" Muñ bóili : "Móro ṭonkáre holodi chihno ochhi." Bóilá káḷore se bholo ṭonkáku áṇi-kori dekhilá. Dekhilá káḷore se ṭonkáre holodi chihno lágichhi. Se constable bóilá : Stesionoku tsálo. Stesionoku goḷu. Muñ dei-thibá ṭonká bholo thilá. Se ḍerá tini thoro bodzái-kori rokhi-thilá. Ebẹ kórṭore thibá roso ṭonká e mudái dekháilá.

DEPOSITION MADE BY THE SECOND WITNESS.

ENGLISH.

On Thursday I took 5 Rupees and 8 annas (with me) in coppers, and changed them at the market. I got rid of my coppers and left the market to return to my village. On my way I passed by the road where the cloth shops are. When I got there Kanu Suáin and Goborá Báriko were buying stuff at a weaver's shop. A bargain had already been struck, and they were all standing about. Afterwards this weaver said: "Give (me) a Rupee, and take the cloth." Goborá Báriko then took a rupee from his money-box, and gave it. After Goborá Báriko had given him the rupee, he (the weaver) tore off the cloth and gave it to him, as also 4 annas 3 pice. After giving it, we went to the fish-shop. The weaver afterwards came to the fish shop and pulled Goborá Báriko, and the two men pulling and shoving each other, returned to the cloth-shop. I bought some fish and taking them with me went off to my village. I saw Goborá Báriko place a Rupee in this weaver's hand. The weaver examined the Rupee twice, and gave him back 4 annas 3 pice.

DWITI'YO SA'KHI' LEKHA'IBA' BA'NGMU'LO.

O'DIYA'.

Gurubáro dino muñ pántso ṭonká dui s'úkáro dábu nei-kori háṭore bhongáili. Móro dábu sorigolá. Háṭoru gáñku jibáku báhárili. Golá beḷoku muñ lugá-pos'orá háṭore goli. Golá beḷoku Kánu Suaiñ, Goborá Báriko ḍerá pos'oráre lugá kiṇutshonti. Mulo tsálo (idiom :) sobu chhiḍi jáichhi. Sethi uttáru ṭonká dei-kori gámontsá né bóli é ḍerá bóilá. Sethi uttáru ṭonká koráṭoru káḍhi-kori Goborá Báriko delá. Goborá Báriko ṭonkaṭie debáru se gámontsáku chiri-kori delá, s'úkáe pois'á modhyo delá. Se delá uttáru áme mátsho pos'orṭháku báhári golu. E uttáru se ḍerá mátsho pos'oráṭháku jái-kori Goborá Bárikoku jhinkilá. E dui lóko jhinká jhinki-hói lugá pos'oraṭháku ásile. Mátsho muñ kiṇithili. Mátsho dhori muñ gáñku báhári goli. Goborá Báriko e ḍerá hátore ṭonká debáro muñ dekhili. Se ḍerá dui thoro dekhi kori se ṭonkáṭi rokhi-kori s'úkáe pois'á delá.

DEPOSITION MADE BY THE THIRD WITNESS.

English.

On Thursday I went to market. This man was bargaining with the weaver about some stuff. Upon my asking him about it, he told me that the price agreed upon was 12 annas. When the weaver asked for the price, this man gave him one Rupee. The weaver rang the Rupee three times, and put it on the cloth. He then took out 4 annas and 3 pice, and gave it to this man. Afterwards the weaver handed Goborá Báriko the cloth and I returned to my village. Goborá Báriko never gave the weaver this bad Rupee. I was quite close. The weaver rang the Rupee three times, and as the Rupee was a good one he kept it and gave him (back) 4 annas 3 pice. It was 4 o'clock at the time.

STATEMENT MADE BY A PRISONER.

The first complainant A'sir Moliko, and I have been on bad terms for four years on account of a dispute about some land. He complained one year to the Collector about the land. The letter of complaint was referred to the Tahsildar of Gumsur. The Tahsildar after inquiry decided the right to the

TRUTI'YO SA'KHI' LEKHA'IBA' BA'NGMU'LO.

O'ḌIYA'.

Muñ Gurubáro dinore háṭoku ási-thili. E ásámi se ḍerá lugá mulo koru-thile. A'me e ásámiki potsháribáru e ásámi kohilá: "E lugá bárá oṇá helá." Ḍerá khortso mágibáru e ásámi se ḍeráku ṭonkáṭie khortso delá. Ḍerá se ṭonkáṭi tini thoro bodzái-kori se gámontsá upore rokhilá. Ḍerá s'úkáe pois'á káḍhikori e ásámiki delá. Se úttáru se ḍerá Goborá Báriko..u gámontsá dei pokáilá. Se uttáru muñ móro gáñku báhári goli. E roso ṭonká Goborá Báriko se ḍeráku dei náhiñ. Muñ pákhore thili. Se ḍerá tini thoro ṭonkáku bodzáilá. Bholo ṭonká hói-thibáru rokhi-kori s'úkáe pois'á táku delá. Sete beḷoku tsári ghonṭo somoyo hoi-thilá.

KOIDI' LEKHA'IBA' BA'NGMU'LO.

Prothomo dábádáro A'sir Moḷiko móro tsári borshoṭháru bhúmi bishoyore biruddho hói-ochhi. Góṭáe borsho boḍo Sáhebongkoṭháre e bhúmi bishoyore dábá korithilá. Sodoro dábá orjí Ghumsuro táhásildárongkoṭháku indárso korá-golá. Táhásildáro doriyápto kori sodoro bhúmi móte

ENGLISH.

land in my favour. He made a second and a third complaint to the Tahsildar. The Tahsildar neither accepted them nor listened to him. The following year he made a complaint before the court at Aska, but they would have nothing to say to it. From that day up to the present time, Asirá and I have been on bad terms. Meanwhile in the month of June last, the Forest Overseer came to Dorpingiá and other villages and told me that I must point out to him the trees that had been cut down in the fields. Accordingly I took two other persons with me, and went to inspect the fields, and after inspecting them, we measured their length and breadth and counted the large trees. (The overseer) then appointed us three persons as his witnesses, and upon receiving summonses from the Tahsildar we repaired to Russellkonda. The Tahsildar then fined all persons, who had cut down the forest trees three rupees each. In consequence of the enmity between Asir Moliko and myself, he and I do not speak up to the present day. Asir Moliko is trying to ruin my reputation, and has deceitfully appeared against me as a witness to prove that I got him punished, and that he has given me a bribe (*i. e.* paid me money) for the express purpose of depriving me of the very land for which he formerly sued me. I have never taken his money. He was also on bad terms with me for some time, because I got his brother fined for clearing land, and

ṅoko kole. Se dwitíyo thoro trutíyo thoro táhásildárongkoṭháre dábá kolá. Táhásildáro grohoṇo kole náhiñ ki s'uṇile náhiñ. Tohiñ áro borsho A'siká kórṭore dábá kolá. Tángke modhyo s'uṇile náhiñ. Se dinoṭháru áji porjyonte A'siráku móte biruddho hói-ochhi. Ethimodhyore goto "June" másore Forest Overseer hebá sáhebo Dorpingiá ogáirá grámoku ási móte kohileki: "Podorománongkore thibá gots-hománongku háṇibá bishoyore tu ámbhoku dekháibáro ochhi," bólibáru muñ áu dui dzoṇongku dhori podorománongku dekhibáku golu. Podorománongku dekhi táro lombo ós'áro mápilu boḍo boḍo gots-hománongku goṇilu. A'mbhe tini dzoṇongku sákhí rokhile. Táhásildáro somoṇo koribáru sákhi-rúpe Russellkoṇḍáre hádzoro helu. Jómáne boṇo gots-ho háṇithile semánongku táhásildáro proti dzoṇoku tini ṭonká lekháre dzorimáná kole. A'sir Moḷikoku móte épori biruddho thibáru áji porjyonte táro móro kothá náhiñ. Jeuñ bhúmi bishoyore dábá hói-thilá, se bhúmi A'sir Moliko nóṭháru ts-hoḍái nebáku upáyo kori sákhi hói muñ doṇḍo diái delá pori móte ṭonká modhyo delá pori, móte boḍonámo deuchhi. Muñ ṭonka nei náhiñ. E podorománe háṇibá bishoyore áuri táro bháiku dzorimáná koráibá sokás'u muñ bondhá rokhithibá duiṭá bilo Dodziáku muñ kiṇili bóli mó sángore kete dino biruddho hói rohithilá. Sumáru tini borsho toḷe Dodziá tsóri koribáru dhorá poḍilá.

ENGLISH.

also because he thinks that I bought the two fields that were mortgaged to me by Dodziá. About three years ago Dodzia was caught for stealing. At that time the Police Deputy asked me to assist him in the case, which I did. For these reason Dodziá complains against me, but from the 12th of September I was employed as a road gumasta and I never said one word about any order having come from the Collector, nor did I frighten him. What they say about having given me money is false. The Kondhs have three or four times put their heads together to drive me out of the village of Dorpingiá. Three people in Russellkonda heard them say that if Krishna Sau did not pay them back the amount of fine that they had paid, that they would charge him with taking money from them. Again, last year I went to plough my field, and Dodzia assembled some Kondhs in order to beat me, and the Kondhs came out and abused me and said that if I ploughed the land again they would kill me. I ploughed the land however and then came away. Out of spite for this they have brought this charge against me, but I neither asked them for money, nor went to their village. When I was road gumasta, I stayed in Bodimá village for three or four months, but I never once had any conversation with Bishnu, nor did I either obtain any money from him, nor ask him for any.

O'ḌIYA'.

Sethire "Police" "(Dipiṭi)" Deputy. "Ehi tsóri nomberore tu móte kumbhoko koro" bólibáru muñ kumbhoko koli. E bishoyománongku sokás'u Dodziá mó upore dábá korichhini "September" máso báro tárikho logáitoru muñ "road" gumástá páiṭire thili. Boḍo Sáhebo hukumo ásilá bóli muñ kohi náhiñ, semánongku ḍorái náhiñ. Ṭónká móte deinántini mits-ho kohuts-honti. Dorpingiá grámoru móte ghouḍi-debáku Kondhománe tini tsári thoro ekoṭháre dzomá hói kóthábárttá houthile. Dzorimáná diáithibá ṭonká Krishṇo Sáu ámbhoku no diáile ámemáne táku ṭonká deithilá pori dábá koribu bóli Russellkonḍáre kothábárttá héuthibáro tini dzoṇo s'uṇi-otshonti. A'uri modhyo goto borsho muñ podoro tsosibáku góṭáe dino sokáḷe jáu-thili. Se Dodziá móte máribáku kete dzoṇo Kondhománongku dzomá kori rokhi-thile. Muñ tsosibá somoyore Kondhománe báhári móte gáli kole: "A'u thore tsosile tóte háṇibu," bóli kohile. Muñ podoro tsosi báhári ásili. Ehi hiñgsá rokhi dábá korutshontini muñ tángku ṭonká mági náhiñ ki tángkoro gáñku jái náhiñ "road" gumástá hói-kori Bodimá grámore tini tsári máso rohili. Bishṇu songe móro kebe kothábárttá náhiñ, muñ táháṭháru ṭonká áṇi náhiñ ki mági náhiñ. Bálingiá rohoṇi Moḷiko ogáirá móṭháru borshoku borsho dháno ruṇo néu-thibáro. Se ruṇo mágibá páñre muñ thore jái-thili. A'uri móro iláká lóko-

English.

In Balingiá village, Moliko and others are in the habit of borrowing corn of me from year to year, and I have been thither to dun them for my debt. My people have also been thither from time to time to ask for it. This year the above named Moliko cut down a big jungle, and the whole village built themselves new houses. Upon my reporting this circumstance to the Forest Overseer, the forest peons went and interfered, and Moliko has a grudge against me as he knows that I reported it, but I neither took any money from him, nor did I ask him for any. If I had taken money from the Kondhs when they cleared the land of trees, would I have informed the Overseer about their having done so? I gave information to the Overseer about all the land that they had cleared. The Overseer told me to report any clearing to him and accordingly I did so, otherwise it was no business of mine. After the Kondhs had been fined, I informed the Overseer at the some time that they intended to ruin me. They have the whole country on their side, whilst I stand quite alone. It is now twenty years since I built a house in the village, and am supporting myself by farming and trading. They have brought a false complaint against me, but I have committed no offence. Brundhá Sundi knows that Asir Moliko pledged me his land, and that I advanced him money and you can inquire of him. I want to leave Dorpingiá, but as

máne thoroku thoro sodoro dháno mági-jibáro. E borsho sodoro Moḷiko boḍo boṇoku goṭáe háṇi ochhi. Grámo jáko nuá ghoro tóḷi-ots-honti. E songoti Forest Overseer sáhebongku dzoṇá koribáru sodoro Overseer sáhebongkoro páikománe jái Kondhománongku tákíto kohibáru muñ dzoṇáilá porire bódho kori móṭháre hirshá rokhi kohu-ochhi. Muñ táṭháru ṭonká néi náhiñ ki mági náhiñ. Muñ jebe Kondhománongkoṭháru gots-ho podoro háṇibá sokás'u ṭonká nei-thánti bóile, Forest Overseer sáhebongku podoro háṇibá bishoyore kópori dzoṇá koronti? Jete poḍoro háṇuts-honti sobu podoro bishoyo Overseer sáhebongku dzoṇá kori-ochhi. Overseer sáhebo gotsho podoro háṇibá bishoyore ámbhoku dzoṇá kori bólibáru muñ dzoṇá koli, nohile móte-kichhi iláká no thilá. Kondhománongku dzorimáná kolá uttáru móte nás'o koribáku Kondhománe bitsáro koruts-honti bóli sete beḷe eká Overseer sáhebongku dzoṇá kori-ochhi. Semáṇe dés'o jáko éko, muñ goṭie lóko. A'dzoku kóḍie borsho helá se grámore-bándhi tsáso kori bonidzo kori protipóshoṇo héu-ochhi. Emáne mithiyá dábá kori-otshontini muñ dósho kori náhiñ. Bhúmi bondhá rokhi A'sir Moḷikoku ṭonká dei-thibá Brundhá Sundiki doriyá-poto koribáku dzoṇá ochhi. Muñ se Dorpingiáru báhári jibáku itstshá koruchi moro ruṇo dháno ruṇo ṭonká bilo bondhá ṭonká no debáru muñ jái páru náhiñ.

ENGLISH.

they do not repay me my loans of corn and of money, nor the money advanced on mortgage for fields, I am unable to go.

FOURTH PART

OF

A PRACTICAL HANDBOOK OF THE URİẎA OR O'DIYA' LANGUAGE.

LETTERS IN ROMANIZED URIYA AND ENGLISH.

N. B.—The following letters on different subjects will serve to illustrate the epistolary style made use of by the Uriyas. The learner may study the letters with advantage.

1. FIRST LETTER.

English.

The petition of us three persons Benu Behorá, Norosingho Goudo, and Sároti Mohángkudo, is as follows: It is now 21 days since the Berhampore Police sent us hither. We are poor people, and gain our livelihood by daily cooly. The two complainants have given us no batta, and up to the present time at the rate of two rupees a man, we three people have incurred expenses amounting to six rupees. As our children have nothing to eat at home, they must have suffered want. If your honour will therefore give us permission, we will go away to our homes. Moreover we will come and present ourselves on whatever day they summon us. May you graciously be pleased to understand this.

Saturday the fifth day of the bright fortnight, month Bhádropodo, year Kiloko.

2. SECOND LETTER.

From Sri Durgá Mádhobo Singho Deu, zamindar of Bodogodo and Serogodo, salutation :

৬. PROTHOMO ORJI.

O'ḌIYA'.

Benu Behorá. Norosingho Goudo. Sároti Mobángkuḍo ámbhe tini dzoṇo onéko solámo kori lekhibáro hokigoto ki bóile: Borhompuro Polésu (Police) ámbhongku éṭháku poṭhiái ekóis'i dino helá, ámbhe no thibá lóko, ródzo kuli kori poripóśboṇo héu-thibáro, dábádáro duheñ ámbhongku khorṭso deu-náhánti, é soriki dzoṇoke dui ṭongká lekháre tini dzoṇo tsho ṭongká khortso kolu, ámbho ghore pilámáne kháibáku no thái klés'o páu-thibe, é heturu khámondo silo dele ámbhe báhári jibu. Punorpi jeuñ dino ḍokaile se dino ási hádzoro hebu.

Dibyo obodhánoku áṇibá hebe.

Kiloko námo sombotsoro Bhádropodo s'uddho pontsomi s'onibáre.

৯. DWITI'YO ORJI.

S'ri Durgá Mádhobo Singho Deu dzomídáro táluko Boḍogoḍo áṇdu Serogoḍongkoro solámo orji.

ENGLISH.

I have duly received your letter No. 20, dated the 26th November last, favouring me with a passport in order to proceed to Sri Juggernath, and have made myself acquainted with its contents. I informed your honour, however, that I wished to proceed to Sri Juggernáth in the month of Kartika, but when the passport arrived, the opportunity had passed away, and I was therefore prevented from going. I therefore write to let your honour know this. Be pleased to consider it.

The fourteenth December, 1864.

---

3. THIRD LETTER.

After many saláms the letter which Sri Krushno Tsondro Suro Horitsondono Deu writes is as follows: I am staying here by your honour's orders. The Government peons who are with me, will allow no one to come near me, and give me trouble. At present the feast of Dasara is close at hand, and I ought to perform the customary ceremonies upon its occasion by piling arms. If the peons interfere with my people, the ceremony cannot take place. If the ceremony does not take place, it will be reckoned a sin to me, and I therefore beg that your honour will be pleased to issue orders to the peons not to interfere with my people either going or coming as well as not to prevent my performance of

O'ḌIYA'.

E' uttáru, goto nobomboro máso ts-hobís'i tárikho (kóḍie) ୨୦ nomborore S'ri Dzogonnáthongku dors'ono kori jibá nimitte doyá koribá ráhádári hukumo probés'o hói sethíro songoti bódho helá, hele Kárttiko másore S'ri Dzogonnáthongku dors'ono koribáku ámoro bántshá thibáru khámondongku dzoṇa koráibáro hóithilá. Ráhádári hukumo ásibá soriki jibáku káḷo byobodhi no thibáru protibondhoko hebáku protikároṇo helá. Ihá khámondongko dzoṇá nimitte lekhilu. Khátoroku áṇiba hebe.

(୧୮୭୪) Oṭhoro s'o tsoushoṭhi sombotsoro Disomboro máso (୧୪) tsobis'i tárikho.

---

୩. TRUTI'YO ORJI.

Srí Krushṇo Tsondro S'úro Horitsondono Deungkoro onéko solámo kori lekhi ghenibá orji, ki bóile: Khámondongko silo prokáre ámbhe eṭháre otshu. A'mbhoṭháre thibá sorkáro páike ámbhoṭháku káháku no tsháḍi, áṭonko koru-otshonti. Borttománoro Mohádukhá uts-hobo somípo helá. Ethoku ámbhe hotyárománongko bosái bidhi bidháno tsoláibáku ochhi. Páike lókongku áṭongko kolá pokhyoku se bidháno tsolibo náhiñ. Bidháno no tsolile sethiru ámbhongku protyobáyo hebo, é swokás'oru prárthoná koribáro, ki bóile, ámbhoṭháku já áso hebá lókongku áṭongko no kolá porire ámbhe tsoláibá uts-hobo bidhánoku modhyo áṭongko nohilá porire modhyo, paikongku khámondo phoromási ámbhongku somoro-

the customary festival, and that you will be pleased to grant me this favour.

Besides this, owing to my remaining here my means are exhausted, and I have much difficulty in meeting my daily expenditure. As I have no friends in the place, I am unable to borrow any money. I therefore beg that your honour will take pity upon me. Be pleased to consider it.

---

4. FOURTH LETTER.

After salutation, the letter which Sri Durgá Mádhobo Singho Deu, zamindar of the taluks of Bodogodo and Serogodo writes, is as follows: Both my estates are covered with forest, and tigers, bears, and other wild beasts constantly inhabit it. If therefore my peons go about without guns, swords, bows and arrows, etcetera, whether when with me, or when going about amongst the villages, it will be exceedingly dangerous for these people. Moreover on the road which I have to travel to Serogodo, there is a great deal of jungle, and if these people do not carry their arms, my own life might perhaps be in danger. Besides, when I go into the Maliahs, if they do not carry arms, it will be impossible to get on. It is for this reason that when your honour was on your way to the Maliahs, I made the fact known to you at Surada. I therefore beg that your honour will grant me your entire favour, and be pleased to issue the

khyoṇo koribá hebe. E báháre ámbhe eṭháre thibáru khortso sorijái dinokrutyo tsolibáku bohuto koshṭo hói-ochhi. Poritsoyo no thibá dzágá hebáru eṭháre ruṇo modhyo milu-náhiñ. E' swokás'u khámondo ámbhongku somorokhyoṇo koribáku prárthoná koru otshu. Chittoku ánibá hebe.

---

४. TSOTU'RTHO ORJI.

S'rí Durgá Mádhobo Singho Deu dzomidáro tálu-ke Bodogoḍo aud Sérogoḍongkoro solámo ki hóile: Ámbhoro dui rádzio bohuto oroṇyo des'o byághro bhálúkádimánongko sontotore thibáro é héture ámbho páikáli lókománe ámbho pákhore thibá káḷore ki ámbho grámománongko bulu-thibá somoyore ki noḷi khoṇḍá káṇḍo báuñgs'ádi hotyárománongko oti práṇo bádhá hebo puṇi áme Sérogoḍoku jáuthibá somoyore báṭore oti boṇománongkoṭháre s'ostro no thibo, tebe ámbho práṇoku modhyo bádhá ási pároi, áuri máḷoku jibá somoyore sodoro hotyárománe no thile tsoli no pároi. E sokás'u je khámondo máḷoku proyáṇo koribá somoyore Sórodá goḍoṭháre dzoṇá koráibáro hói-thilá. E héturu khámondo ámbho upore púrṇo onugroho rokhi é ámbho dui tályká ṭesonománongku (stations) ki ámbho námore ki hukumo doyá koribá nimitte bitsári otshu. Khátoroku áṇiba hebe (୧୮୨୪) Oṭhoro s'o tsoushothi sombotsoro (Feb-

necessary orders in my name and also to the station houses in my two taluks. Be pleased to consider it.

The 18th February, 1864.

---

5. FIFTH LETTER.

After many salams, the letter which Lakshmi Narayana Pat Naik, an inhabitant of the town of Parla Kimidi, writes, is as follows :

Whilst I was discharging the duties of head writer, which is hereditary in our family, in the service of Sri Ràjah Jaganath Gajapathi, and supporting myself along with my family, your honour dismissed me, and as nine months have now passed since I was brought to head-quarters as a prisoner, and the tenth month has begun, the soukars who lent me a thousand rupees refuse to give me credit any longer, and cause me much annoyance. The women and children, forty souls in all, also suffer much for want of food and clothing. Moreover my aunt has rheumatism, my elder sister has diarrhœa, and my wife has fever, and as there is no one to help them, and give them medicine, it seems as if they must die. Besides the twenty-first day and night of my son's birth is near at hand. For this reason and on account of the water and air here not agreeing with my body, and causing my stomach to swell, and giving me rheumatism, I beg that your honour who is just, generous,

O'ḌIYA'.

ruary) Pebruori máso ୧୮ (oṭhoro) tárikho.

---

୫. PONTSOMO ORJI.

Párolá Kimundi páṭoṇá rohoṇi Lokhhmi Náráyoṇo Potonáyoko onéko solámo kori lekhi ghenibá orji ki bólonte : S'rí Dzogonátho Godzopothi mohárádzáng-ko tshámore ámo purushánukromore heḍ (head) gumástá noukorire thái sokuṭumbo sométore poripóshoṇo heu tháu khámondo móte borotoropho kori hodz'uruku oṇái ádzoko no máso jái dos'o máso helá. Koidí rúpore rokhibáru hodzáro ṭonká ruṇo debá sáukárománe modáro háṇi kori bohuto áṭonko koru-otshonti. Tsális'i práṇi strí báḷoko orno bosroku bohuto áyáso héu ochhi, puṇi mó sáno máku báto bedoná mó ópáku grohoṇi bédoná mó bhárjyáku dzworo émánongku oushodho dei somorokhyoko ke no thibáru ogotyore práṇo golá-porire dis'u ochhi. Mó puoro ekois'i rátro dino modhyo somipo hói-ochhi, é bitsároṇoru é páṇi é pobono mó dehoku no jái peṭo phulá báto bedoná hói-ochhi. Ethi károṇoru nyáyo korttá hebá dhormós'ílo hebá doyábonto hebá bibekotwo hebá e dibidzoṇore poromés'woro hebá khámondo tsális'i práṇi kuṭumboku práṇo dáno dei somorokhyoṇo koribá páñre onugroho rokhi sonátonore thibá mo noukorire mui rohi poripóshoṇo hebá nimonte hukumo doyá koribá

merciful, clever and all powerful in this division will be pleased to give orders to restore me to my ancient office, and by granting me support will be pleased to protect my family of 40 persons and grant them their lives.

Be graciously pleased to consider it: Tuesday the 2nd day of the dark fortnight, month Srabana, year Kiloko.

---

6. SIXTH LETTER.

After many salams, the letter which Narayano Ráyo Guru, an inhabitant of the Fort of Surada writes is as follows: On the 8th of this month as I was not worthy to visit your honour, I wrote a letter, and made known to you the ups and downs of my previous condition. You will (doubtless) have taken it into your consideration, and I now beg to state, that formerly we enjoyed a good reputation in our family, and supported ourselves by trading, but as at present I have no work, the time passes in great distress (for me.) Formerly your honour gave me work for some days in Surada as peshkar, but as I have no work at present, I only stay at home in great distress and do nothing. I therefore beg that your honour, who is a father to me, will take compassion upon me, and grant me employment any where in some capacity attached to a zamindary taluk, in order that I may earn my livelihood. (I promise) to

páñre onéko prárthoná koru-ochhi. Dibyo chittoku áṇibá hebe.

Kiloko námo sombotsoro s'ráboṇo s'uddho dwitíyá Mongolobáre.

---

୨. SHOSHṬOMO ORJI.

Sároḍá goḍo rohoṇi Náráyoṇo Ráyo Guru onéko sôlámo kori lekhi ghenibáro orji ki bóile: E máso átho tárikhore khámondongko dors'onoku jógyo nóhi móro púrbo sthiti koshṭo sukho modhyo orji góṭie lekhi dzoṇá korái-thili, tohiñru dibyo chittoku ási-thibo. Ebe muñ dzoṇá koráibáro ki bóile, púrboru móro purushánukromore boḍo lókopoṇo thibáru byoboháro éká brutti kori poripóshoṇo héu-thibáru é soriki kichhi páiṭi no thibáru bohuto koshṭore káḷo nemáro poḍu-ochhi. Móte modhyo khámondoghoro Sóroḍá pes'káro páiṭi thókáe dino dei thibáru páiṭi tsoláu-thili, ebe páiṭi no thibáru ghore eká bohuto dukhitore bosi rohi-ochhi. Ethoku mábápo hebá dhormosworúpo khámondo móṭháre doyá kori kóṭháre hele dzomidáro táluká sombondho páiṭi góṭie doyá kole muñ poripóshoṇo hebi. Mó hátore ribiṇi (revenue) páiṭi uttomo hói tsolibo. Khámondo borsho góṭie mátro dekhile muñ sorkáro páiṭire tsolibá

discharge the revenue work in first rate style, and if your honour will try me for a year, your honour will recognize the manner in which I perform the work of Government. If your favour is not with me in the matter which I write about, I have no other refuge, neither have I any other means of gaining my livelihood. By my bad luck I have not had any opportunity of waiting upon your honour.

Be pleased to consider it.

The 22nd September, 1848.

NARAYANA RAYA GURU.

---

7. SEVENTH LETTER.

Sri Biro Sri Birádhi Biro Protápo Sri A'dikondo Onongobhimo Debo Kés'ori, Zamindar of the Toluk of Protapogiri, presents his compliments and (writes) as follows: I have received your firmán, dated the 23rd October, telling me to despatch a true report of what had happened, with regard to the defendant Lokonátho Suain, and others who had had a quarrel with Lotshomono Dolo Behorá, the renter of Pentho village in the Taluk of Protapogiri and other petitioners, about some land with the crop standing on it, which the latter had rented to the former, and I have made myself acquainted with its contents, as well as with those of the letter you enclosed therein. The true facts of the case are as follows: It is quite true that Lotshomono Dolo

proborttoná khámondongku protyokhyo hebo. Muñ lekhibá bishoyore mótháre koṭákhyo nohile móro ános'orono náhiñ. Móro durádrushṭo sokás'u khámondongku onus'orono koribáku káḷo durghoṭoná héuochhi. Muñ bohukuṭumbi hebá sokásu onus'orono jogyoko hói náhiñ. Ebe dors'onoku upékhyá kori ási-ochhi. Dibyo chittoku áṇibá hebe.

୧୮୪୮ (oṭhoro s'o oṭho tsálís'i) sombotsoro Sopoṭomboro máso ୨୨ (báis'i) tárikho.

NA'RA'YONO RA'YO GURU.

---

୭. SOPTOMO ORJI

S'rí Bíro S'rí Birádhi Biro Protápo S'ri A'dikondo Onongobhímo Débo Kés'ori Mohárádzá Dzomidáro Táluke Protápogiringkoro solámo ki bóile: Protápogiri táluká Penṭho grámo mustádáro Lotshomono Doḷó Behorá ogáirá orjidárongku gutáku deithibá bhúmire hebá phoḷosáyoko mudái Lokonátho Suáiñ ogáirámáne durnoyo koruthibá-pori ethi bishoyore ki tsoli ochchiki sethiro nidzo sthiti dzoṇá koráibáro ochchi bóli ákoṭoboro (October) ୨୩ (téis'i) tárikhore lekháibá phorománá biḍái orji múloru modhyo jábonto songoti protyokhyo helá. Ethiro nidzo sthiti kemonto bóile orjidároku Protápogiri Penṭho mustádáro Lotshomono Doḷo Behorá ogáirá sodoro dábá bhúmi jiráyitire gutá dei-thibáro soto. E bhúmi Penṭho sombondho jiráyiti bhúmi ekáni Dzogon-

ENGLISH.

Behora and others, who are renters of Pentho village in Protápogiri, have rented the disputed land on ryotwar tenure. The land in question is ryotwar attached to the village of Pentho, but has nothing at all to do with the land on the Jagannathapur side. Upon their bringing their case before me in the matter of the aforesaid disputed land, I assembled a "panchayet" some days ago, and passed a decision to the effect above recorded. I beg therefore to report the matter for your honour's information by this letter, and to return at the same time the letter that you enclosed.

May your favour rest upon me and may you be pleased to consider it.

The 18th November, 1863.

---

8. EIGHTH LETTER.

After many saláms, the letter which Narayono Rajendro Patro, Sirdar of the Chinna Kimidi Maliahs writes, is as follows:—About a month ago the villages of Mesi, Rabopoli, Radzo, Gerdzongo and some 20 or 30 other Kondh villages in the Manru country, which is under the Pánigonda chieftain in my district, began a disturbance, and as it appeared to me they were preparing to fight, the head men of the Muthá, inhabitants of Gulubá village, *viz*. Bhokto Pátro, and Podono Behorá Dolai gave information to Tsokro Behorá and to Dolái Lotshomono Madola,

náthopuro iláká bhúmi kete mátroko náhiñ. Sodoro dábá bhúmi bishoyore ámbhoṭháre dábá áṇibáru ámbhe toḷo dine pontsáito korái upore lekhá hebá prokáre tírpu korái ots-hu. E songoti khámondongko dzoṇá nimitte orji múlore nibedono korái biḍái muñ orji modhyo poṭhiáibáro helá. A'mbhoṭháre doyá rokhi khátoroku áṇibá hebe.

୧୮୬୩ (oṭhoro s'o téshoṭhi) sombotsoro nobomboro máso ୧୮ (oṭhoro) tárikho.

---

୮. OSHṬOMO ORJI.

Sáno Kimundi Máḷo sordáro Náráyoṇo Rájendro Pátro onéko solámo kori lekhi ghenibáro mánibi orji ki bóile :—

Mó iláká Pánigoṇḍá godiá toḷe Mesi Kábopoli Gerdzongi e ogáirá romáromí kóḍie tiris'i khoṇḍo grámoro Kondhománe ádzoku másoko toḷe durnoyo dzáto kori gheni juddho koribá páñre árombho kori ghenilá pori sethi bishoyore se muṭhá odhikárostho hebá Gulubá grámo rohoṇi Bhokto Pátro, Podono Behorá Doḷái se des'o odhikárostho hebá Pánigoṇḍá grámo rohoṇi Tsokro Behorá Doḷái Lotshomono

inhabitants of Madolá and the head men of that ilk, and proceeded to the spot in question, in order to try by all manner of means to put a stop to the disturbances. In spite of their efforts, however, the Kondhs of the said village would not desist, and after pulling down their houses, they left for the mountains. In a battle which took place, four Kondhs were killed, and one man wounded, and although the aforesaid Bhokto Pátro and Podono Behorá Dolái did their best to put a stop to the disturbances, they were unable to do so. Immediately upon their coming and informing me of the matter, I sent off a letter and the two individuals in question to your honour. Large numbers of Kondhs from the Maliahs, attached to the Bodogodo side, have also joined these Kondhs. I therefore begged in my letter that your honour would take the matter into your consideration and come here, as it would then be easy to put a stop to the disturbances. I also gave written instructions to all the fort-holders that if any outrages took place of a criminal nature, they were forthwith to send a written report of the same to Russellkonda. In accordance with these instructions, they have been in the habit of acting without fail from that time to the present, but whether in the present instance they have reported matters or not, I am not aware. I myself have received no information from them until now, but I now beg to report what I know to your honour in this letter.

Be pleased to consider it.

The 21*st February*, 1863.

O'ḌIYA'.

Mádoḷátháre dzoṇá koráibáru semáne sodoro bibádo stholoku jái kete rúpe proyotnore dwondománongko nibároṇo koráile modhyo no nibortti ghorománongko bhángi dei porbotománongku sodoro grámo Kondhománe báhári gole. Juddho koribáre tsári dzoṇo Kondho mori-gole góṭie Kondho modhyo ghá hoi poḍi-ochhi, áme kete rúpe niborttáile modhyo, se dwondo kete mátroko nibortto hói párilá náhiñ bóli sodoro Bhokto Pátro, Podoni Behorá Doḷái ási móṭháre dzoṇá koráibá tokhyoṇore s dui dzoṇo ásámiki é orji sáthe khámondongko hodzúruku poṭhiái dei ghenili. Se Kondhománongko sáthe modhyo Boḍogoḍo iláká Máḷo sombondho bistáro Kondhománe misi ots-honti. E sokas'u se dwondo nibároṇo hebáro sádhyo khámondo tokhyoṇore bitsároṇoku áṇi ásoi bóli orji múlore nibedono kori ghenili, áuri modhyo móro íláká goḍiámánongku tumo ḍés'ománongkore Mejistret (magistrate) iláká kouṇosi khuṇímánongko tsolibá soriki tokhyoṇore Rosúlokonḍáṭháku bokíro múlore dzoṇá koráibáro ochhi bóli somosto goḍiámánongku tákído korái-thili. Se prokáre modhyo se logáitoru ádzo 'soriki niráṭonkore tsoli ásuthilá. Borttománo sethi bishoyore se ásámimáne sepori bokíro dele-ki náhiñ móte dzoṇá náhiñ. Móte modhyo é soriki bokíro dei no thile. Móte dzoṇá hebáru é songoti khámondongko hodzúruku tokhyoṇore orji múlore nibedono kori ghenili. Dibyo chittoku áṇibá hebe.

Oṭhoro s'o teshoṭhi sombotsoro (୧୮୭୩) Pibrobori (February) máso ekóis'i (୨୧) tárikho.

ENGLISH.

The signature of Narana Rajendro Pátro, Maliah sirdar (a title).

---

9. NINTH LETTER.

The petition of Dzonárdono Pátro, who is performing the duty of Karnam in Khásopágodo in the Bodogodo Táluk, is as follows: I have neither land nor wages attached to my office of Karnam. I used (formerly) to receive yearly russooms in the shape of one adda of paddy for every bharnam of land from the cultivating ryots and Inamdars, as well as other articles. Besides this, ryots subject to the moturpha tax, and the merchants of the place used to give me a rupee or twelve annas for each house, but for the last two years, owing to the Government having abandoned the collections of the Moturpha (tax), all these people have proved refractory and will not pay me my fees. For the last five years also the inamdars have paid me nothing, either in the shape of paddy or other things. As the ryots did not pay me, I presented two petitions to the Collector, but got no answer to them. I have also informed your honour personally two or three times of the fact, and have presented petitions besides, but owing to my bad luck, it was all of no use. I therefore write this letter to you. This place is a fort, and if I do not stay here, and always do my work, I cannot exist. If I don't get any food, how am I to do my work? I therefore beg

O'ḌIYA'.

Máḷo sordáro, Náráyoṇo, Rájendro Pátrongkoro hostákhyoro.

ι. NOBOMO ORJI.

Bodogoḍo Táluká Khásopágoḍo rohoṇi koroṇiko páiṭi tsoláuthibá Dzonárdono Pátrongkoro lekhi ghenibá bokíro ki bóile: Móro koroṇiko sombondhoku bhúmi podoro ki borttono ki kichchi náhiñ. Tsáso koribáro roitongkoṭháru inámodárongkoṭháru bhúmi bhoroṇoku rusumo dháno oḍáe lekháre jiniso modhyo é onukromore borshoku borsho miḷuthái. E báháre modhyo mohontorophá roito Peṇṭho mohádzománongkoṭháru ghoro góṭike ṭonkáe tsho s'úká lekháre deuthánti. A'dzoku dui borsho helá Sorokáoghoro mohontorophá tsháḍi dele, bóli é jábonto lóke meduároporo kori rusumo dou-náhánti. A'dzoku pántso borsho helá inámodárománe modhyo rusumo dháno ki jiniso rúpe kichchi deu náhánti. E pori roitománe no debáru máhárádzo s'ri Kolekoṭro, (Collector) sáhebongkoṭháre dui orji modhyo dei ghenili. Sethiki kichhi jobábo mililá náhiñ. A'poṇongkoṭháre modhyo sákhyátore dui tini thoro kohi orji modhyo dákholo kori ghenili, hele móro odrushṭoku kichhi phoḷilá náhiñ. E héturu ápoṇongko soriki lekhi ghenili. Eto goḍo dzágá sobu beḷe rohi noukoro no kole áyotto náhiñ. Móte jebe ádháro no thibó, muñ kópori tsoláibi. E heturu ápoṇo mó upore doyá kori mohárádzo s'ri Kolekoṭro

your honour to represent the whole facts of the matter to the Collector, and if I only receive my customary fees, I shall always continue in Government employ, and do my work. If, however, I cannot obtain my food in this manner, I will with your permission gain my livelihood in some other way, for I cannot continue in the office of Karnam. What more can I write to one so learned as yourself?

Be pleased, Sir, to consider it.

The 15th June, 1863.

---

10. TENTH LETTER.

To T. J. Maltby, Esq., Assistant Collector, in the District of Ganjam.

After many salams the letter of Gongá Ráui Náyoko, Karnam of Grisolá village of the Kodiá Muthá in the Taluk of Ghumsur, as in follows: Since I was confirmed in the office of Karnam in the above-named village, I have carefully discharged my duties. In Fusly, 1279, in consequence of the Tahsildar ordering me to measure the above-named villages, I did so in obedience to his orders. After measuring the village a hundred rupees were added to the Government revenue, and in consequence of this excess of 100 rupees, the Kárji, and all the ryots argued that the Karnam had made the measurement, and had reported that they were liable in the sum of 100 rupees, as excess to Government. Accordingly the aforesaid Kárji and the ryots (lit.

sáhebongkoṭháku é jábonto sthiti dzoṇá kori móto rusumorobiso diáibá pokhyoku muñ soḍá káḷe Sorokáro noukorore rohi páiṭi tsolái ghenibi. E pori ádháro no mililá soriki, móte silo dele muñ kóporire hele poripóshoṇo hói ghenibi. E koroṇo páiṭiki muñ páribi nahiñ. A'poṇoto gyátosáro odhiko ki lekhibi. Dibyo chittoko áṇi obodháno hebe.

Oṭhoro s'o teshoṭhi (୧୮୬୦) sombotsoro Junu máso pondoro tárikho.

---

୨୦. DOS'OMO ORJI.

Mohá rádzá s'ri si-ji-Máltibi iskoyoro Gondzámo jilá A'sishṭánṭo Kolekoṭro sáhebongko hodzúruku. Ghumsuro táluká Koḍiá muṭhá Grisolá grámo koroṇo Gongá Páṇi Poṭo Náyoko onéko solámo kori lekhi dákholo kori ghenibá orji ki bóile: Sodoro grámo koroṇiko páiṭire móte mokoráro hebáṭháru muñ jukto prokáre páiṭi tsolái ghenu-thili. Sonno bárá s'o onás'i (୧୨୮୯) phoslire sodoro grámo noḷibáro ochhi bóli tohosildáro pondite hukumo koribáru sodoro hukumo prokáre muñ sodoro grámo noḷili; sodoro grámo noḷibáru sorkároku jástire s'ohe ṭonká bosilá. Jásti s'ohe ṭonká bosibáru sodoro grámo kárji jábonto roitománe bóile koroṇo noḷi korisiná sorkároku ámbho námore sorkároku jástire s'ohe ṭonkáku lekhá delá bóli sodoro kárji porodzámáne ékotbo hói móṭháre irshá kori muñ sodoro grámore thile modhyo no thilá

subjects) agreed amongst themselves to spite me, and wrote letters to the Tahsildar of the Táluk informing him that I was not in the village, although I was there all the time. From July to December, 1872, the demarcation and the whole survey of the village took place. If during this time I was not present in the village, how could the work have been performed? Whilst I was constantly in the village the Karji and ryots conspired together against me, and reported to the Tahsildar that I was absent from it. The Tahsildar made no inquiry into the matter, and after reporting me to your honour, dismissed me. Subsequently the Tahsildar recommended the Senior Assistant Collector to appoint a cutcherry peon named Rengea to the office of Karnam in the aforesaid village. Your honour, however, inquired into the matter and confirmed me in the office. In consequence of my being confirmed in the office of Karnam, the Tahsildar was displeased with me. For this reason he has three times since written to your honour, and recommended that I should be dismissed. I therefore pray that your honour will inquire into the whole matter and give me back my office. Moreover since I have been confirmed in the office of Karnam, I have never done anything wrong, and the ten members of our family who feed on Government rice and water, performed the work of Government, and we gained our livelihood thereby. Owing, however, to the loss of my office, we ten people have become helpless. If therefore your honour will recommend me for Govern-

pori táluká tohosilodáro ponditongkoṭháku bokíro lekhu-thánti. Oṭhoro s'o bástori sombotsoro Juli máso logáitu Disemboro máso porjyonte sodoro grámo dimárkesoṇo helá, sorbo noḷo helá, e monmodhyore muñ grámore hádzoro no thile sorkáro páiṭi ko-pori tsoliláki? Muñ grámore hádzoro tháu tháu mó námore kárji porodzámáne ékotbo hói tohosilodáro ponditongkoṭháku muñ grámore hádzoro no thilá pori riporṭo dele. Se kotháku tohosilodáro pondite doriyápto no kori mó námore khámondongko hodzúruku lekhi borotoropho kole. E uttáru sodoro grámo koroṇiko páiṭire tohosilodáro pondite kocheri páiko Rengeá námore sodoro grámo koroṇiko páiṭi deḅáro ochhi bóli máhárádzo s'ri Senioro Asishṭánto Kolekoṭro sahébongkoṭháku lekhithile. Dhormo sworúpo hebá khámondo é kotháku doriyápto kori mó námore mokoráro kole. Mó námore koroṇiko páiṭi mokoráro koribáru tohosildáro ponditongkoro móṭháre nionugroho tháe, é héture khámondongko hodzúruku mó námore é modhyore tini dophá lekhi borotoropho koribá páñre s'upároso kole. E' jábonto kothá dhormo sworúpo hebá khámondo doriyápto kori móro páiṭi móte debáro ochhi bóli onéko prárthoná koru-ochhi. E' uttáru muñ koroṇiko páiṭire mokoráro hebáṭháru sorkáro páiṭire kebe hele khuṇí kori náhiñ. Sorkáro ornodzolo khái sorkáro páiṭi kori dos'o práṇi kuṭumbo poripóshoṇo heuthilu. Jebe móro páiṭi jibáre dos'o práṇi kuṭumbo hinosthá helu. Ethoku dhormo sworúpo hebá khámondo áu kóṭháre hele sorkáro páiṭire mokoráro helá pori s'upároso dele

ment employment in some other place, my family of ten persons will be able to gain a livelihood and manage to exist. On the other hand, however, if your honour raises his arm against us, we shall become helpless and have to subsist by begging.

---

11. ELEVENTH LETTER.

After many salams the letter which Sudarsana Poto, Karnam of Kumunda village in the muthá of Jaganath Prasád in the Taluk of Gumsur, writes is as follows: Owing to certain ryots of the aforesaid village, viz. Mongolo Podhano, Jogonatho Podhano and the rest of them, cultivating waste land without first making an application for it, and my entering the same in the accounts after measuring it; owing to my increasing the assessment by measuring the village in Fusly 1280 and to my giving information to Government against those persons who did not pay the tax due for removing valuable timber; owing to my reporting to Government the names of those persons who threw rubbish into the street; owing to my distraining the property of those ryots, who did not pay their arrears upon the appointed date of the assessment falling due; owing to my having reported to the late Tahsildar that Hori Naik, a Samastána Paik of the village had dug a well at the foot of the bund recently repaired, thereby damaging the tank bund, and owing to the Tahsildar causing the well to be filled

ámbhe dos'o práṇi kuṭumbo protipóshoṇo hói poritháponá hói rohibu, nohile dhormo sworúpo hebá khámondo báhu ṭeki-dele hinosthá hói-mági khái-jibu.

୧୧. EKA'DOS'O ORJI.

Ghumusoro táluká Dzogonáthoprosádo muṭhá Kumundá grámo koroṇo Sudors'ono Poṭo Náyoko onéko solámo kori lekhi dákholo kori ghenibáro orji ki bóile modzukúru grámo roitománe hebá Moṇgolo Podháno, Dzogonnátho Podháno, Bonomáḷi Podháno e ogáirá doróbosto ásámimáne dorkhásto no-kori bonddzoro ságumánongko koruthibáru proti sombotsorore muñ noḷi lekhá dákholo koribáru (୨୮୦) báro s'o os'ie phosolire, grámo noḷi s'istu jásti koráibáru ó pánu Sorkárore dákholo no kori khorído hebá káṭhománongko áṇibáre muñ Sorkáruku dzoṇá koráibáru, dáṇḍore kátsorománongko pokáithibáre se bishoyore Sorkároku riporṭo (report) koribáru, s'istu osúlo koribá biṣhoyore báidá prokáre ṭongká no debáru roitománongkoro tsorásti dzopti koráibáru, morámoto huḍá toḷore sodoro grámo somostáno páiko Hori Náyoko góṭie kúoñ khóḷáibáre morámoto bondho huḍáku háṇi ásibáru leṭo (late) tohosildárongkoṭháre riporṭo koribáre, se khóḷáithibá kúoñku pótái debáru, sodoro ásámiṭháre upárdzono bishoyore sorkároro nirnoyo korithibá Indiáno inkongtánsu (Income-tax) prokáre

up in consequence; and lastly owing to my imposing the tax upon the earnings of the same individual with reference to the Indian Income Tax Act, passed by Government; for all these reasons, the aforesaid people bear me a grudge, and for some years past have brought false complaints against me. At present, in consequence of my having made a charge against these ryots five months ago for throwing down rubbish, they assembled in one spot (lit. sat down), and after some of them had agreed to be the complainants, and others the witnesses, they asserted: firstly, that I had secretly cultivated land bearing an assessment of three annas; secondly, that I had embezzled Government revenue because I had accidentally omitted to insert any date in a receipt; and lastly, the complainants and their shepherds gave evidence that I had embezzled the pound dues collected from the shepherds, because I had prevented the ryots' female buffaloes from trampling down the bund recently repaired by Government. The persons who were witnesses in the first case, then became complainants in the second, and deposed that the Karnam had pledged his Inám land for ten rupees, because I had allowed the first complainant Jogonátho Prodháno to cultivate part of it, and in order to prove this, they produced a forged document made by the complainants, and to which they themselves were the only witnesses, and although neither I nor my divided brother had executed the document, owing to the name of the person who wrote the document not appearing

pánu pokái-thibáre é somosto bishoyománongko muñ koráili bóli, sodorásámimáne mó upore hirshá bóhi goto sombotsorománongkore kolpito dábámánongko koruthibáru, borttománe muñ ádzoku pántso máso toḷore kátsorá bishoyore sodoro roitománongku dósháróponọ koráithibáru; koroṇoku kolpito dábámánongko dwárá éhi prokáre nomborománongko (number) kori borotoropho koráibá bóli góṭie stholore bosi, thókáe lókománe dábádáro hói, thókáe lókománe sákhyo hebá bóli promáṇó kori prothomore tini oṇáro bhúmi muñ tshopáuṇi korithilá pori poropáṭore góṭie tárikho rosídore (receipt) no poḍithibá héturu sorkáro s'istu opohoroṇo korithiláporire, sorkáro morámoto huḍá roitománongkoro mohiñshí tsokuṭibáre muñ oṭoko koruthibáru tángko iláká goudománongkoṭhâru doḍi dzorimáná osúlo kori opohoroṇo koruthilápori prothomo dábádárománongko goudománe sodoro dábádárománe rudzu hói-otshonti. Prothomo orjire s'ákhi hói-thibá ásámi dwitíyo orjiki dábádárō hói koroṇo inámo bhúmiru ṭikie bhúmi prothomo dábádáro Dzogonnátho Prodhánoku mun bhágo tsosibáku deithibáṭháre dos'o ṭonkáku muñ tonokhá deithilápori mó upore kolpito dostábedzo góṭie kori dábádárománe eká sákhi hói, sodoro dostábedzo muñ no lekhi deithibáṭháre móro bibhokto hói-thibá bhái modhyo no lekhithibáṭhare ámbhe dui dzoṇo thóke thóke lekhi deithilá porire sodoro dostábedzo lekhibá lókoro námo no thái muñ eká sobu lekhi deithilápori dostábedzore drushyo korái rudzu hói-otshonti. Sodoro bhúmi jebe dábádároku muñ tonokhá dei thánti, tebe

ENGLISH.

upon it, they asserted that I had written the whole of it, so as to appear as if my brother and myself had each of us consented in part. Had I really mortgaged my land to the first complainant, why would the complainants not have informed the Government of it in the first complaint that they brought against me? With regard to this fact I informed the Tahsildar that I would prove that the complainants had conspired against me, but without paying any attention to this, he never wrote the matter in my statement, nor examined the witnesses whom I called, and without paying the slightest attention to what I said, he accepted the story of the complainants as perfectly true. I therefore beg that your honour will be pleased to take compassion upon me, and after calling for the records of the cases inquired into by the Tahsildar, that you will ascertain all the circumstances connected with the complaints preferred against me, and reverse the sentences passed upon me.

The 25th January, 1873.

The signature of,

SUDORSONO POTO NAYOKO.

---

12. TWELFTH LETTER.

After many saláms the letter which the renter, the ryots and other persons in the taluk of Gumsur beg to present is as follows: Up to Fusly, 1223, Rajah Dho-

dábádárománe prothomore mó námore áṇibá dábáre sorkároku dzoṇá korái no thánteki? Ethire dábá-dárománe góṭie stholore bosi promáṇo koribá songotiki muñ sáḳhi rudzu koráibi bóli tohosildáro ponditongku kohibáru e bishoyo chittoku no áṇi mó koiphetore no lekhile mó toropho sákhimánongku bimorshá no kole kébolo dábádárománongko kothá nis'tsoyore ghenile, muñ kohibá kothá kete mátroko chittoku no áṇile. Ethoku dhormosworúpo hebá khámondo mó-ṭháre doyá rokhi tsolito nomborománongkore tohosil-dáro nirdés'o korithibá gronthománongko oṇái mó námore tsolithibá jábonto songoti kópori tsoḷi ochchiki bitsároṇo kori ásithibá dábámánongko niṣhedho koráibá páiñ prárthoná koru-ochchi.

୨୫ (Ponchis'o) tárikho Jonobori (January) máso ୧୮୭୦ (oṭhoro s'o téstori) sombotsoro.

SUDORSONO POTO NA'YOKO HOSTA'KHYORO..

---

୧୨. DWA'DOS'O ORJI.

Ghumusoro Táluká mustádzoro roito ógáirá somosto lókománe onéko solámománongku kori lekhái dákholo kori ghenibáro orjiḳi bóile: Sonno bárá so téis'i

ENGLISH.

nurdzoyo Bhondzo reigned in the above taluk. Owing to the rajah however having probably misconducted himself, and the matter coming to the knowledge of Government, Mr. —— came to this taluk accompanied by an army, and took the rajah prisoner. The Government then placed the aforesaid taluk under "amani" tenure, and Dili Ochuto Rámo became manager, and transacted the business. Formerly Dyáno Poto Náyoko, who was diwán to the Rajah, and Rotono Prodháno had managed the country and were acquainted with all the affairs of the Kondh Maliahs attached to the taluk. In Fusly 1226, two persons named Dorá Bisoi and Báhu Bolindro began to create disturbances and after first killing Rotono Prodháno and Dyáno Poto Náyoko, they caused disturbances throughout the country and in three days' time burnt all the villages of the taluk, killed and beat the people, and plundered all their property. The people of the taluk then abandoned all that they had and fled to the different taluks of Dosopolá, Nuágoḍo, Aṭhogoḍo, Dhorakóṭo and Sorodá, and there we abode. For a whole year, we remained in these taluks, suffering much distress. In the meanwhile the people who had caused the disturbances got hold of a female child and pretending that it was the rajah's son Boḷo Bhodro Deu, they made it rajah. The Government, however, detained Rajah Sri Koro Bhondzo at Bhábopuro (Bápur). The rajah having left that place by some means or other, came to Durgáprosádo, and having summoned the people, who had caused the disturbances, to the place,

phosoli soriki modzukúru tálukáre Sri Dhonur
zoyo Bhondzo rodzá rádzotbo koru-thile. Sodoro rodzá keuñ ojyukto songoti tsoláibáru obá Sorkároghoroku jáhéro poḍibáru —— Sáhebe é tálukáku loskoro dhori ási se rodzángku dhori nele. Sodoro táluká Sorkároghoro ománi toḷe rokhi Dili Ochúto Rámo Pondite menodzoro (manager) hói bujhu-thile. Toḷo dine sodoro rodzángkoghoro pátro hói thibá Dyáno Poṭo Náyoko, Rotono Prodháno é dui dzoṇo muloko bujhi e tálukáre jábonto kondho maḷo jáko jáhéro korithile. Sonno bárá s'o tshobis'i (ﺳﻮﺭ) phosolire Dórá Bis'ói, Báhu Bolindro é dui dzoṇo phituri koribáku, árombho kori se Rotono Prodháno Dyáno Poṭonáyoke é dui dzoṇongku ạdyore háṇi des'o phituri kori tini dino bhitore é táluká proti grámo póḍi lókongku háṇi mári jábonto podártho lúṭi kole. Sodoro tálukáro ṣomosto lóke jábonto sorboswo tsháḍi pái táluká Dos'opolá, Nuágoḍo, A'ṭhogoḍo, Dhorákóṭo, Soródá e tálukámánongkore jái rohilu. Boroshe porjyonte se tálukámánongkore dukho koshṭo poḍi rohi-thilu. E' bhitore se phituri koribá ásámimáne máikiniá pilá góṭiku rodzángkoro puo Boḷo Bhodro Deu bóli táñgku semáne rodzá kori ghenithile. S'ri Koro Bhondzo rondzangku Sorkároghoro Bhábopuroṭháre rokhithile. Seṭháru sodoro S'ri Koro Bhondzo rodzá kóprokáre ási Durgáprosádoṭháku gole. Phituri korithibá lókománongku seṭháku ḍokái Boḷo Bhodro Deu Bóli jeuñ máikiniá piláku rodzá koruthile ṭángku oṇái máikiniá pilá bóli nis'tsoyo bujhi Sahebongkoṭháku poṭhiái dele. Se uttáru Tákeri Sáhebe Nuagáñṭháku ási sodoro Sri Koro Bhondzo rodzángku

and sent for the female child, whom they had made rajah, he ascertained its sex, and forwarded the child to the gentleman. Subsequently Mr. Thackeray came to Nuágán, and after summoning Sri Koro Bhondzo the rajah, he made over to him the estate, and sending for the people who had fled from this and the other taluks, he entrusted them to the rajah's care, and departed. During the fourteen years that the rajah reigned, besides affording us every protection, he allowed no thefts, disturbances, or other misdemeanours to take place, and we lived in great comfort. After this, in Fusly 1242, the Government brought forward Dhonondzo Bhondzo as rajah, and gave him the estate, and upon their detaining rajah Sri Koro Bhondzo at the shrine of Purushottomo, Dhonurdzo Bhondzo reigned as rajah for three years. Upon his incurring the displeasure of Government by some misconduct, the rajah through fear fled to the Maliahs, upon their bringing an army into the country, and having summoned all the paiks of the taluk, he gave them strict orders not to fire upon the Government troops. In the meanwhile the Government troops advanced and encamped at Galeri. Up to that time not a single bullet had been fired. The riotous people though who had formerly caused the disturbances disobeyed the rajah's orders, and fired upon the troops. The rajah hearing that his people had disobeyed his orders, and fired upon the Government troops was grieved, and departed this life in the Maliahs. Those people then plundered all the wealth

ḍokái áṇi rádzotbo dei pái tálukámánongkoru é tálukáru poḷáithibá podháno roito ogáirá lókongku ḍokái áṇi rodzángkoṭháre somorpoṇo kori dei se sáhebe báhári gole. Sodoro rodzá rádzotbo koribáre tsouḍo borosho porjyonte roitongku uttomo protipáḷoṇa koribá báháre, tsóri méḷi ogáirá kouṇosi upodrobo no thái uttomo sukhore thilu. E uttáru sonno (bárá s'o boyális'i) phosolire Sorkároghoro Dhonondzoyo Bhondzo rodzángku áṇi rádzotbo dei Sri Koro Bhondzo rodzángku S'ri Purushottomo khyetroro rokháibáre sodoro Dhonurdzoyo Bhondzo rodzá tini borosho rádzotbo kole. Tángkoro keuñ durjógoru Sorkároghoroṭháre biródho koribáru Sorkároghoro e mulokoku loskoro aṇimá káḷore se rodzá bhoyore máḷoku báhári jái é táluká páiko somostongku ḍokái kohile: Sorkároghoroku kete mátroko guli máribo náhiñ, bóli moná kole. Ethire Sorkároghoro loskoro nei Gáleriṭháre pokáile. Se porjyonte kóṭháre hele guli phuṭi no thilá. Rodzangko hukumoku no máni toḷo dine phituri korithibá sehi meḷiá lóke punorpi guli márile. E lóke móro hukumoku no máni Sorkároghoroku guli márile, bóli bismoyo hói sodoro rodzá máḷore bijógo hói-gole. Rodzángkoro thibá dhono drobyo jábonto se lóke lúṭi kori nele. Táluká póḍi bhángi punorpi Sorkároghoroku modhyo guli márile. E uttáru mohárádzo S'ri Rosulo Sáhebe bistárore loskoro dhori ásile. Sodoro Dhonondzoyo Bhondzo rodzángko puo hebá Brodzo Rádzo Bhondze sokuṭumbo sometore Nuágáṇṭháre Rosulo Sahebongkoṭháre ási somorpoṇo hele. Sodoro Brodzo Rádzo Bhondzoku puruṇá Ghumusoro-

and property that the rajah possessed. They burnt and plundered the taluk, and fired besides upon the Government troops. After this the Honourable Mr. Russell advanced with a considerable army. Brodzo Radzo Bhondzo, the son of Rajah Dhonondzoyo Bhondzo then came to Nuágan together with his family, and gave himself up to Mr. Russell. Mr. Russell detained him in old Gumsur, and taking the troops with him, he went over the Maliahs and investigated matters, hanging some of the rebels, and transporting others as prisoners to some other country. The Government also deported Brodzo Radzo Bhondzo from the country, and detained him elsewhere. After a tahsildar had been appointed to the taluk, no disturbances took place, and for some time we lived in peace. Mr. Russell also protected us ryots, and in order that no disturbances might occur, he allotted Inam land to the Sirdars, Naiks and Paiks of the taluk, 1500 men in number. In Fusly, 1256, the former rebels and the people attached to them joined together, and commenced disturbances, burning the villages, and killing and plundering. Owing to these disturbances, the General advanced into the country with an army, and whether owing to the influence of certain persons, or because he thought it right, he released the persons who had been confined in the prison at Nuágán for taking part in the disturbances with the other rebels. Upon their being released, these people lost all fear, and by burning the villages, killing the people, plundering our property, and

ṭháre rokhái, Rosulo sáhebe des'o máḷo loskoro dhori buli jáhero kori phituridárománongku dhori phás'i dei, thókáe lókongku modhyo kó des'ore néi bondimáno kori rokhile. Brodzo Rádzo Bhondzongku é des'oru néi Sorkároghoro kó desore rokhái, e tálukáre Tohosildáro rokháibáre thókáe dino porjyonte ámbhe somosto lóke kouṇosi upodrobo no thái nis'tsonto hói rohithilu. Rosulo Sáhebe modhyo ámbho roito lókománongko somorokhyoṇo páiñ punorpi keuñ káḷoku phituri no thilá pori bitsári, e tálukáre somostáno sordárománe náyoko páikó ୧୫୦୦ (eko hodzáro pántso s'o) dzoṇo épori inámo bhúmi dei nirnoyo kori thile. Sonno ୧୨୫୭ (bárá s'o tshopono) phosolire púrbo meḷiá lókománe táṅgkoro iláká lókománe misi phituri árombho kori grámománongko póḍi háṇi lúṭi kole. E'pori phituri hebáru "Dzonorolo" Sáhebe loskoro dhori é des'oku ásile. Keuñ lókongko múloru keuñ nyáyo bujhileke, e phituri korithibá lókoru kete lóko dhori Nuágañṭháre bondire rokháithile ki se lókománongku tsháḍidele. Tsháḍi debáru se lóke nirbhoyo hói é soriki tini borsho helá náná durnoyománongku tsolái grámománe póḍi lókománongku háṇi podártho lúṭi kori bis'eshore upodrobománongku tsoláu thibá héturu táluká ámbho somosto lókongkoro kouṇosi swosthiyo no thái práṇoku bhoyo hói jáháro jeuñ brutti byobosáyománongko modhyo nis'tsontore no tsoḷi ye tápotroyore nás'o jibáru kárоṇo héu ochhi. E' uttáru se phituri lóke jeuñ grámoku jái póḍi háṇutshonti seṭháre bolutshonti: Táluká lóke Sorkároghoroṭháre kohi rádzotbo koráo, nohile tumoro práṇo podártho kouṇosi ás'á páibo náhiñ.

ENGLISH.

committing numerous other misdemeanours, they have caused all sorts of trouble for the last three years. We people in the taluk are all of us without any security and are afraid for our lives. Owing to no man moreover being able to follow his trade or profession in peace, we are reduced to the last extremity by this accumulation of evils. Moreover the rebels after coming to a village and burning it, and killing people, say to the others: "If you people in the taluk don't go to the Sirkar, and beg of them to set up the Rajah, neither your lives nor your property will be safe." They also state openly that the Rajah's child is with them. For three years past, these troubles have not been put a stop to, and now that they are constantly repeated, the lives of all the people are in danger. We therefore humbly pray that your honour taking into consideration the safety of the people, will determine, whether it is better, as it appears, to put a stop to this accumulation of evils by restoring the Raj in order that we may live in peace; or, if this course does not commend itself to Government, that either troops may be sent, or other steps taken in order to take all these rebels prisoners, so as to allow of a stringent enquiry being made, in order that a repetition of these troubles may never again occur, and in order that we may henceforth continue to live in peace.

Be pleased to consider it.

The 22nd December, 1848.

O'ḌIYA'.

Tángkoṭháre modhyo rodzá pilá ochhi bóli phukáro koruotshonti. A'dzoku tini borsho helá é upodrobo nibároṇo nohi punoḥ punore hebáru ámbho somosto lókongko práṇo upore poḍilá. Ethiswokás'u dhormo sworúpo hebá khámondongko hodzúrore jáhéro kori gheniméro ki bóile: é tini borshore Sorkároghoro modhyo é phituri nibároṇárthore proyotnománongko kolá uttáre modhyo, é soriki nibároṇo nohilá, é héturu ámbho somosto lókongko somorokhyoṇoku bitsári khámondo dibyo chittoku áṇi é táluká rádzotbo koráibá soriki é tápotroyo nibortti ámbhe sukhore rohilá pori dis'u ochhi, othobá Sorkároghoro ongikároku epori no ásibá soriki, loskoro áṇi obá áu kó prokáre obá, é phituri korithibá jábonto lókongku dhori áṇto doriyápoto kori, áu keuñ káḷoku hele kete mátroko kouṇosi durnoyo no tsolibápori ámbho somosto lókongku sukhitore rokháibá pañre onéko prárthoná koru-otshu. Dibyo chittoku áṇibá hobe.

୧୮୪୮ (oṭhoro s'o oṭhotsális'i) sombotsoro ḍisemboro máso ୨୨ (báis'i) tárikho.

FIFTH PART.

A PRACTICAL HANDBOOK OF THE URIYA OR O'ḌIYA' LANGUAGE.

Ni'ti Kotha' or Moral Fables.

1. THE DEER AND LION.

ENGLISH.

Once upon a time a deer ran away through fear of a hunter, and entered into a cave. A lion afterwards caught the deer there and killed it. Then the deer as it was dying began to say: "Alas! what a misfortune has happened to me; in fleeing from the hand of man, I have fallen into the hand of an enemy more powerful than he."

The moral of this is, that if a man does not act carefully, it may so happen that in fleeing from one danger, he will fall into another danger still more dreadful.

2. THE HARE AND THE TIGRESS.

A hare approaching a certain tigress exclaimed: "O tigress listen, whilst I produce a numerous offspring yearly, you from your birth until your death do not bring forth more than one." The tigress then said: "The solitary offspring which I produce is worth more than your numerous ones."

The moral of this is, that one good son is better than many bad ones.

୧. MRUGO A'U SINGHO.

O'ḌIYA'.

Kouṇosi somoyore góṭie mrugo byádho bhoyore poḷái eko gortto bhitore probés'o helá. Tohiñ uttáre góṭáe singho seṭháre táháku dhori bodho kolá. Tohiñre se mrugo moroṇo somoyore kohibáku lágilá. Háyo! háyo! ámbhoro ki durghoṭoṇá helá, ámbhe monushyo hátoru poḷái táháṭháru odhiko boḷobonto áu eko s'otru hátore poḍilu. Iháro tátporjyo ehi, sábodháno hói no tsolile emonto ghoṭe ki monushyo eko ápodoru poḷái tohiñru odhiko bhoyánoko onyo ápodore poḍe.

୨. ṬHEKUA' A'U BA'GHUṆI'.

Góṭie ṭhékuá kouṇosi bághuṇí nikoṭoku jái kohilá: He bághuṇí suṇo, proti borsho ámbhoro onéko sontáno huonti, mátro tumbhoro dzonmo obodhi moroṇo porjyonte góṭie sontánoru odhiko dzonmonti náhiñ. Tohiñre bághuṇí kohilá: ámbhoro jeuñ eko sontáno hue, se tumbho onéko sontánoṭháru s'réshṭho.

Iháro tátporjyo éhi, onéko odhomo sontánoṭháru eko uttomo putro bholo.

3. THE WOMAN AND THE GOOSE.

ENGLISH.

A certain woman kept a goose which laid every day a silver egg. Then the woman said to herself: "If I increase the goose's food, it will perhaps lay at the rate of two eggs daily." With this desire she began to give it more food than previously, but owing to the goose's stomach becoming swollen with excess of food, it died.

The moral of this is, that the man who is desirous of excessive profit loses even his previous gains.

4. THE MOSQUITO AND THE BULL.

A mosquito sat on a bull's horn, and, in its pride imagining that it was heavy, said to the bull: "If you feel tired by my sitting upon you, pray say so, and I will fly away to some other spot." The bull said: "O mosquito, I had not even the slightest idea that you were sitting upon me."

The moral of this is, that he who prides himself upon his own renown and prowess will speedily suffer shame.

᱕. STRI' A'U HONGSI'.

O'ḌIYA'.

Kouṇosi strí góṭie hongsí póshe. Séi hongsí proti dino éko éko rupáro ḍimbo prosobo kore. Tohiñre se strí mone mone kohilá : A'mbhe jebe é hongsíro áháro boḍhái debu, tebe proti dino dui dui ḍimbo lekháe obá páḍibo. E'hi ás'áre se táháku púrboṭháru odhiko áháro debáku lágilá, mátro jothéshṭo bhódzonore hongsíro peṭo pháṭibáru se mori golá.

Iháro tátporjyo éhi, monushyo odhiko lábho itstshá kori áponaro púrbo punji suddhá noshṭo kore

᱖. MOS'A' A'U BRUSHO.

Góṭie mos'á éko shoṇḍo s'rungo upore bosi ohonkárore áponáku bhárí bujhi shoṇḍoku kohilá : A'he shoṇḍo ámbho bosibáru jebe tumbhoku bhári láge, tebe koho, ámbhe onyo sthánoku uḍi jáuñ. E' kothá s'uṇi brusho kohilá : A're mos'á tu je ámbho upore bosi ots-hu, é kotháro ṭerosuddhá pái náhuñ.

Iháro tátporjyo éhi : Jeuñ lóko áponá khyáti ó protápore obhimáno kore, se bege lodzdzá páe.

5. THE MAN AND DEATH.

ENGLISH.

A man who was carrying a faggot of sticks along, got very tired as it was heavy, and throwing down the faggot began to pray for his death. Then death approaching him said: "Tell me, why are you calling me?" Hearing these words the man said: "I called you that you might place this faggot upon my head."

The moral of this is, that all desire to dwell in the world, and lo! even though a man be very old and unfortunate, yet scarce any one wishes for death.

6. THE TORTOISE AND THE HARE.

Once upon a time a tortoise and a hare making the top of a mountain their goal, said: "Come let us see which of us two will arrive there first." Hereupon the two began to run. The hare owing to its being slender, light, and swift was boastful, and went to sleep in the middle of the road; but the tortoise being heavy and slow, was afraid, and not delaying on the road was the first to ascend the mountain. The hare afterwards arose from its sleep and seeing that the tortoise had got there first, was much ashamed.

The moral of this is, that if there be a contest be-

୪. MONUSHYO A'N MRUTYU.

O'ḍIYA'.

Dzoṇe monushyo káṭho gótshá gheṇi jáuñ jáuñ bhárí hebá heturu otis'oyo klánto hói, se bódzho pokái delá, áu áponá mrutyu prárthoná kolá. Tohiñre mrutyu táhá nikoṭore uposthito hói kohilá : Tumbhe kipáñ ámbhoku ḍákilo bólo. E' kothá s'uṇi monushyo kohilá : E'hi bódzho ámbho mundoku uṭhái debá nimonte ḍákiluñ.

Iháro tátporjyo éhi : Pruthibí modhyore somoste bonchibá páiñ itstshá·koronti. Dekho, oti bruddho ó duḥkhí heleheñ práyo kéhi mrutyu tsáhe náhiñ.

---

୬. KOTSTS-HOPO O' ṬHE'KUA'.

Kouṇosi somoyore kotsts-hopo ó ṭhékuá é duheñ éko porboto s'rungoku lokhyo kori : A'so ámbho duhinko modhyoru kie áge ṣeṭháre pohunchi páribo, éhi kothá kohi duheñ douḍibáku lágile. Ṭhekuá pátoḷo áu loghu áu begogámí hebáru ohonkárí hói potho modhyore nidrá golá ; mátro kotsts-hopo bhárí ó mondogámi hebáru bhoyo kori potho modhyore nidrá bis'rámo no kori áge porbotore uṭhilá. Onontore ṭhékuá nidráru uṭhi dekhilá kotsts·hopo áge jái-ochhi, tohiñre se boḍo lojjito helá.

Iháro tátporjyo éhi. Boḷobán áu durboḷo e duhinko

tween a strong man and a weak one, it is very improper for the strong man to be careless, because by the neglect and carelessness of a powerful man, a weak one is able to gain the victory.

---

7. THE THORN TREE.

A thorn tree said to a gardener: "If any one were to take the trouble to plant me in a garden, and water my roots every day, then kings would certainly desire to see my flowers and fruit." The gardener accordingly took it, and planting it in a fertile spot in the middle of the garden, watered it twice every day. By so doing the thorns of the tree all increased in strength, and owing to its boughs and branches extending, the trees that grew on all four sides of it, all perished; afterwards its roots grew by degrees, and the tree overran the whole garden. Finally no one could go near it on account of the thorns.

The moral of this is, that if you give shelter to a bad man and protect him, his evil disposition will only increase, and should you do him a kindness he will only do you an unkindness in return.

---

modhyore juddho hele boḷobánoro osábodháno hebáro oti onuchito, károno ki boḷobáno lókoro héḷá áu áḷosyo héturu boḷohíno dzoyí hói páre.

---

9. KOṈṬA' BRUKHYO.

Góṭie koṇṭoko brukhyo dzoṇe máḷiku kohilá : Jodyopi kéhi ámbhoku jotno kori bogicháre róporo korontá ebong protidino ámbho múḷore páṇi diontá tebe rádzámáne obos'yo ámbho phuḷo pholo dekhibá nimonte cheshṭá koronte. Tohiñre se máḷi táháku gheni bogichá modhyore phoḷobonto sthánore róporo kori proti dino dui thoro páṇi debáku lágilá. E'hi rúpe koribáru se brukhyoro koṇṭá sobu boḍhi s'okto helá, áu táhá tsári pákhore jete brukhyo thile se somostonko upore dáḷo s'ákhá boḍhibáru sei sobu brukhyo noshṭo hele. Tohiñ uttáre krome krome táháro chero bruddhi hebáru, se gotsho bogichá jáko beḍhi golá ; obós'eshore koṇṭá 'lági kehi táhá nikoṭoku jái párilá náhiñ.

Iháro tátporjyo éhi : Dushṭoku ás'royo dei jete táháro somádoro koribo tete táháro dushṭo swobhábo boḍhe, áu jete táháro upokár okoribo tete se phér'iopokáro koribo.

---

8. THE BLACK MAN.

English.

A black man took his clothes off and smeared his body over with chunam. A certain person thereupon asked him: "Why do you smear your body over with chunam?" Hearing this, he answered: "I am smearing my body over with chunam in order to get white." The other man thereupon said: "O black man, do not give your body unnecessary trouble, for although you may be able to make the chunam on your body black, yet chunam can never remove your own blackness."

The moral of this is, that a bad man may make a good man bad, but no one can ever make a bad man good.

9. THE LION AND THE TWO BULLOCKS.

A lion one day sprang at two bullocks in order to kill them, but the two bullocks keeping together would not allow the lion to get between them and struck at him with their horns. The lion afterwards played them a trick and said: "O bullocks, if you will separate, I will do no harm to either of you." The bullocks relying upon this speech separated, and the lion then killed them both.

The moral of this is, that so long as men remain united, no man's enmity can prevail against them, but once they separate, all will perish.

r. KOLA'BORNO PURUSHO

O'ḌIYA'.

Dzoṇe koḷáborṇo purusho bostro tyágo kori tsuno nei áponá s'orírore leputhilá ; tohiñre kouṇosi lóko táháku potsárilá : A'he tumbhe káhiñ páiñ déhore tsuno lepono koru-otsho ? Ihá s'uṇi se uttoro kolá gouroborṇo hebálági tsuno lepono koru-otshu. Tohiñ uttáre se lóko kohilá : A'he krushnoborṇo purusho, tumbhe áponá dehoku bruthá kles'o dio ná, károṇo ki tumbho s'oríro tsunoku koḷá kori páre, mátro tsuno tumbho koḷáborṇoku ghuntsái páribo náhin.

Iháro tátporjyo éhi : Mondo bholoku mondo kori páre, mátro mondoku bholo koribáro s'okti káhári ṭhare náhiñ.

ɩ. SINGHO A'U DUI BOLODO.

Dine góṭáe singho dui boḷodoku máribá nimonte semánongko uporoku douḍilá ; tohiñre se dui boḷodo ekotro hói, singhoku áponá modhyore ásibáku no dei s'rungore máribáku lágile. Tohiñ uttáre singho tshoḷo kori semánongku kohilá : A'he boḷodománe jebe tumbhe duheñ ologá hói jibo, tebe ámbhe káhári kichchi khyoti koribuñ náhiñ. Se kotháre protyoyo kori boḷodo duheñ bhinno huonte singho duhingku mári pokáilá.

Iháro tátporjyo éhi—Monushyománe jábot ékobákyo hói rohonti tábot sémánongko upore kéhi s'otrutá kori proboḷo hói páre náhiñ, mátro onoikyo helo somoste noshṭo huonti.

10. THE LONG-HORNED ANTELOPE.

ENGLISH.

Once upon a time a long-horned antelope suffering from thirst went to a pond and drank. Then seeing in the midst of the water the ugliness of its feet it was grieved, but on seeing the length of its horns it was pleased. In the meanwhile some hunters approached, and the antelope fled to the open waste land, and the hunters were unable to catch it. Afterwards it entered a dense jungle, and its long horns becoming entangled in the branches of trees and in brambles, the hunters killed it without any difficulty. The antelope as it was dying, regretfully exclaimed: "Alas! alas! the feet which I despised saved me, but the horns of which I was proud have caused my destruction."

The moral of this is that, a man should not enquire whether a thing is beautiful or ugly, but what its use is, and relying upon this, should estimate its value accordingly.

11. THE ANTELOPE.

Once upon a time an antelope was sick, and the friendly and neighbouring animals coming to see it, ate up all the grass both dry and sprouting that grew all round it. After the antelope's sickness had abated, it wished to partake of some food but could find

‥. DI'RGHOS'RUNGO HORIṈO.

O'ḌIYA'.

Kouṇosi somoyore éko dírghos'rungo horiṇo trushåre áturo hói góṭáe dzolás'oyoku jái dzoḷo páno kolá. Todbádo dzoḷo modhyore áponá pádoro ḳhíṇotá dekhi birokto helá, mátro s'rungoro dírghotá dekhi ánondito helá. Ithimodhyore byádhománe' uposthito hebáru horíṇo poḍiáre poḷái golá, áu byádhománe táháku dhori párile náhiñ. Tohiñ uttáre se nibiḍo bonore probes'o huonte dírghos'rungo béturu brukhyo s'ákhá ó lotáre tshondi nebáru báṇuámáne táháku onáyásore mári pokáile. Horiṇo moribá beḷe khedo kori ḳohilá : Háyo, háyo, jeuñ pádoku heyogyáno koruthiluñ se ámbhoku rokhyá kolá ; áu jeuñ s'rungo lági ohonkári thiluñ se ámbhoku bodho koráilá.

Ihåro tátporjyo éhi—Kouṇosi bishoyo sundoro ki osundoro ethire bhábonå no kori táháro guṇo kiprokáro, éhi bishoyore drushti rokhi tohiñro múlyo bibetsoná koribáro uchito.

‥. HORIṈO.

Ketebeḷe éko horiṇo píḍito hebáru táháro átmíyo ó poribáriyo pos'ugoṇo táku dekhibá nimonte ási tsári digore s'ushko ó soroso jete truṇo pollobithilá táhá sobu khái pokáile. Horiṇoro píḍáro s'ánto helá uttáru se kichchi áháro koribá nimonte itstshá kolá,

nothing at all to eat and so died of hunger.

The moral of this is, that it is better not to have any relations at all rather than to have foolish ones.

12. THE LION AND BULLOCK.

A lion once intended to kill a bullock, but as the strength of the bullock was considerable, it did not dare to go near it. Afterwards it went to it and said in a deceitful manner: "O bullock, I have killed a fat young lamb, and I want you therefore to come to my house and dine."

The bullock accordingly accepted the invitation, and went to the lion's house, where the lion had collected a quantity of firewood, and some very large vessels. The bullock seeing this returned. The lion then said: "Why do you go back after coming here?" To these words the bullock replied: "I have understood your intention; for a mere lamb such a fuss would not be made, and it is quite evident that your preparations were made for some animal larger than it."

The moral of this is, that to accept the tales of dangerous people as true and to associate with them, is not the duty of wise people.

matro kichchihiñ khádyo páilá náhiñ, tohiñre khyudháre táháro práṇo bijógo helá.

Iháro tátporjyo éhi—Obibétsoko bondhu thibáṭháru borong bondhu no thibáro bholo.

७. SINGHO A'U BOḶODO.

Dine éko singho góṭáe boḷodo máribáku monostho kolá, mátro boḷodoro boḷo odhiko hebá jóguñ táhá nikoṭoku jái párilá náhiñ. Tohiñ uttáre tshoḷore táhá nikoṭoku jái kohilá : A'hó boḷodo, ámbhe góṭáe hrushṭopushṭo meṇḍhá tshuá mári-otshu otoebo itstshá éhi, ki tumbhe áji rátrire ámbho ghore uposthito hói bhódzono koribo. Todbádo boḷodo nimontroṇo swíkáro kori singho áḷoyoku gomono koḷá, mátro singho onéko káshṭho ó boḍo boḍo háṇḍi prostuto kori rokhi ochchi, ihá dekhi boḷodo pheri golá. Tohiñre singho kohilá : tumbhe eṭháku ási kahiñki phéri jáu-otsho ? E kotháre boḷodo uttoro kolá : tumbhoro monostho dzáṇiluñ ; meṇḍhá, tshuá nimonte etádrus'o udyomo sombhobo nuhe, mátro táháṭháru boḍo kouṇosi dzontu nimonte tumbhoro áyódzono bódho hue.

Iháro tátporjyo éhi—Hingsokoro kothá sotyo bóli gyáno koribá áu táhá songe príti koribáro buddhimáno byoktiro korttobyo nuhe.

13. THE LION AND THE FOX.

ENGLISH.

A lion becoming weak from old age was no longer able to capture living animals. On this account he practised cunning for the sake of food and pretending that he was sick, he took up his abode in a cave resolving that if any animals came to see him, he would seize them and eat them in the cave. Afterwards a fox came, and standing at the door of the cave made his obeisance and said : "O king of beasts, how are you ?" The lion then said : "Why do you not come inside ?" In answer to this, the fox said, "Sir, I see the signs of many animals going in, but not a single one of any coming out."

The moral of this is that it is not proper for men to begin any business without reflection.

14. THE LION AND THE MAN.

Once upon a time a lion and a man met each other on a road, and a dispute arose between them regarding their respective strength and prowess. The lion was boastful of its strength and power. Meanwhile the man drew upon a wall the picture of a man grasping the throat of a lion, and laughingly showed it to

৬৩. SINGHO O' KO'KI'S'IYA'LI'.

O'DIYA'.

Eko singho bárḍdhokyo héturu dzorágrosto hói kouṇosi jíbo dzonturo páridhi kori páru no tháe ; e nimonte ápoṇá áháro páiñ tsholo kori mithyáre píḍito lóko pori hói góṭáe guhá modhyore rohilá károno ki, táháro ehi obhiprâyo thilá je, kouṇosi dzontu ámbhoku dekhibá nimonte ásile, tákáku éhi gortto modhyore dhori gráso koṛibuñ. Tohiñ uttáre góṭáe kóki ási gortto dwárore ṭhiyá hói proṇámo-púrboko kohilá : "Hé pos'urádzo ápoṇo kemonto otsho?" Tohiñre singho kohilá : "Tumbhe bhitoroku no áso kipáiñ?" Ihá s'uṇi kókí kohilá : "Hé obodháno ámbhe eṭháku ási oneko ngko probes'o hebáro chihno dekhiluñ, mátro káhári báháro hebáro éko chihno suddhá dekhu náhuñ.

Iháro tátporjyo éhi—Bibétsoná no kori kouṇosi kormore probrutto hebáro monushyongkoro korttobyo nuhe.

৬৪. SINGHO O' MONUSHYO.

Ketebeḷe potho modhyore kouṇosi singhoro songe dzoṇe monushyo bheṭo hebáru sémánongko boḷo áu bikromo bishoyore porosporo bibádo uṭhilá. Singho apoṇá boḷo ó protáporo ádhikyo héturu áhládito helá. Ethimodhyore góṭie singhoro goḷá ṭipi máru-ochchhi, eprokáro dzoṇe monushyoro protimúrtti sei monu-

the lion. The lion then said; "If a lion could draw like a man, the lion would not have allowed the man to grasp the lion's throat, but the lion would be grasping the man's."

The moral of this is, that from a man's own witnesses no one else can make his escape.

---

15. THE SPIDER AND THE BEE.

Once upon a time, a spider said to a bee: "If you will make me your companion, I shall be able to gather honey like you." As it was constantly repeating the same story, the bee consented. The spider accordingly accompanied the bee, but being unable to gather any honey, the bee stung it and killed it. As the spider was dying, it exclaimed regretfully: "Alas! alas! Why did I ever attempt a work which I had not the ability to perform!"

The moral of this is, that if a man does not possess the ability to perform a work and enters upon it, because he thinks himself very clever, the falseness of his representations and his own unworthiness will be made self-evident, and he will reap the fruit thereof.

---

shyo kouṇosi kánthore tshobi lekhi hosi hosi séi singhoku dekháilá. Tohiñre singho kohilá jebe singho monushyo pori chitrokoro hói tháṇtá tebe monushyoku singho goḷá ṭipái déi no thántá, borong singho monushyo goḷá ṭiputhántá.

Tháro tátporjyo éhi—Swopokhyo sákhidwárá kéhi pa o pái páre náhiñ.

. MA'KOḌOSA' A'U MOHUMA'CHHI.

Kouṇosi somoyore góṭie mákoḍosá mohumáchhiki kohilá: " Jebe ámbhoku áponá sohoborttí koribo tebe tumbho pori modhu sontsoyo kori páribu. E' koṭhá punoḥ punoḥ kohibáru mohumáchhi swíkaro kolá. Todbádo mákoḍosá táháro songí hói modhu áṇi no páribáru mohumáchhi táháku náhuḍo phuṭái mári pokáilá. Tohiñre mákoḍosá moroṇo káḷoro mone mone khedo kori kohilá: Háyo! háyo! jáhá koribáku ámbho s'okti no thilá emonto kormo kipáiñ swíkáro korithilu?

Iháro tátporjyo éhi: Jáháro jeuñ kormo koribáku khyomotá no tháe se jebe áponáku oti poṇdito dzáṇi tohiñre probrutto hue, tebe táhá kotháro mithyá áu táhá ojógyotá prokás'o hue ebong táku somuchito phoḷo mile.

---

16. THE YOUNG MAN.

English.

Once upon a time a young man went into a river of his own accord, and not knowing how to swim began to sink. A certain man was coming along the path at the time, and the young man seeing him, called to him to save him. The man then came near and began to abuse the young man for falling into the water. The young man exclaimed "Hulloh! save me first, and abuse me afterwards!"

The moral of this is, that if a friend of yours falls into any danger, rescue him first from it, and you can then abuse him afterwards.

17. THE DOG AND THE FOX.

Once upon a time a dog saw a piece of tiger's skin in some place, and going towards it began to gnaw in with his teeth. A fox then said to the dog: "If this tiger were alive, you would soon learn that the claws on its feet were longer than your teeth."

The moral of this is, that it is not by exposing a strong man to indignities in times of danger, that the prowess of low-born people will be displayed.

৩. BA'ḶOKO.

O'DIYA'.

Kete beḷe dzoṇe báḷoko apoṇá itstsháre nodíre poḍi pohoñri no dzáṇibáru ḍubibáku lágilá. Ehi somoyore pothore dzoṇe monushyo jáu·ochchi. Táháku dekhi séi báḷoko práṇo rokhyárthe táháku ḍákilá. Tohiñre se monushyo nikoṭoku jái báḷokoku páṇire poḍibá heturu bhortsoná koribáku lágilá. Báḷoko kohilá: A'he prothome ámbhoku bontsáo, pots-he bhortsoná koro.

Iháro tátporjyo éhi: tumbhoro kouṇosi átmíyo ápodore poḍile táku se ápodoru áge mukto kori pos'tsát bhortsoná koribo.

৩. KUKURO A'U KO'KI'.

Keṭe bele eko kukuro kouṇosi stháṇore khoṇḍe byághro tsormo dekhi nikoṭobortti hói táku dántore kámóḍibáku lágilá. Todbádo góṭie kókí kukuroku kohilá: Jebe éhi byághro sojíbo thántá, tebe tumbho dántoṭháru táhá hátóro nokho boḍo, ihá tumbhe dzáṇonto.

Iháro tátporjyo ehi:—S'oktimáno byoktiro bipodo káḷore táháku ákromoṇo koribáru khyudro lókoro bíropoṇo prokás'o hue náhiñ.

18. THE BELLY AND THE BODY.

ENGLISH.

The belly and the body had a dispute between each other about supporting and protecting the body. The body said : " It is I who by my own individual strength carry the body." The belly answered : " If I did not take food, you would not be able to carry anything."

The moral of this is, that no one should despise another, for every one has it in his power to render a mutual kindness.

---

19. THE SUN AND WIND.

A wager arose between the sun and wind to see which of the two would first be able to make a man part with his cloth. The wind accordingly began to blow with great velocity, and the man to protect himself against it, wrapped his cloth round his body. The clouds afterwards dispersed, and the sun began to shine with great power; as he felt very warm, and the cloth was heavy, the man removed it from his body.

The moral of this is, that the wishes of gentle people are more likely to be accomplished, than those of strong but unstable men.

---

৮. UDORO A'U ONGO.

O'ḌIYA'.

Udoro ó ongo e duhingko modhyore s'oríro bohibá áu rokhyá koribá bishoyore bibádo huonte, ongo kohile: A'mbhemáne áponá áponá s'oktire s'oríroku bohu-otshuñ. Udoro uttoro kolá: Jebe ámbhe kichchi áháro no koruñ, tebe tumbhemáne kichchi bohibáku no páro.

Iháro tátporjyo éhi:—Kéhi káháku tutstshogyáno koribo náhiñ, károno ki, somoste porosporo upokárí hói páronti.

৯. SU'RJYO O' POBONO.

Súrjyo pobono duhingko modhyore ehi pono helá: A'so dekhi ámbho duhingko modhyore kie monushyoku bostro tyágo korái páre. Tohiñre báyú otis'oyo begore bohibáku lágilá, áu monushyo táháṭháru rokhyá páibá nimonte áponá bostro dehore ghóḍáilá. Tohiñ uttáre megho sobu uḍi golá, bádo súrjyo tedzo protsoṇdorúpe prokás'o helá; tohiñre monushyo otyonto gríshmo héturu áponá bostroku bhárogyáno kori déhoru káḍhi pokáilá.

Iháro tátporjyo éhi:—Tsontsoḷo boḷobánṭháru susthiro lókoro obhipráyo sohodze siddho hue.

20. THE TWO COCKS.

English.

Two cocks had a fight about some thing. One of them remained the conqueror, and the other one ran away. Then the one who was victorious perched itself on a very high straw-rick, and boastfully flapping its wings, began to crow proudly. A hawk in the meanwhile perceived it, and swooping down upon it, carried it off.

The moral of this is, that he who boasts of his own prowess will quickly be put to shame.

21. FABLE OF CERTAIN HYÆNAS.

Certain Hyænas who saw a cow's hide in a cave wanted to eat it, but the cave was full of water and the hide was nowhere near the edge. Thereupon they all of them with one accord reflected amongst themselves that if they first drank up the water and drained the cave dry, they would be able to get at the skin and eat it. Having come to this resolution, they drank water until their stomachs were full. Owing to their drinking so much water, however, their stomachs burst, and they all died. Moreover they were not able to eat the hide at all.

The moral of this is, that the counsels of people of little sense is profitless.

৯০. DUI KUKUḌA'.

O'ḌIYA'.

Dui kukuḍá kouṇosi drobyo lági juddho kole. Tohiñre góṭie dzoyí helá,ároṭá polái golá. Todbádo je jiṇi tháe, se eko oti utstso páḷogodá upore bosi áhládore ḍená dzháḍi ḍáki ohongkáro koribáku lágilá. Tonmodhyore eko bádzo táháku dekhi dzhámpo mári gheni golá.

Iháro tátporjyo éhi :—A'poṇá porákromore ohongkáro kole s'íghro loḍzdzá hue.

৯৯. KETEKO HEṬA'BA'GHO.

Keteko heṭábágho eko gorttöre gótsormo dekhi táhá kháibáku monostho kole ; mátro sei gortto páṇire poripúrṇo thilá, áu tsormo suddhá tíro nikoṭore no thilá. Tohiñre semáne oikyo hói ehi porámors'o kole : A'so somoste áge dzoḷojáko pánó kori gortto sushko korilu todbádo tsormo gheni kháibu. E' kothá sthiro kori semáne udoro purṇo hebá porjyonte dzoḷo piile ; mátro ete páṇi piibáru somostongkoro peṭo pháṭi mrutyu helá, sutorám tsormosuddhá khái párile náhiñ.

Iháro tátporjyo ehi : Olpobuddhi lókongkoro porámors'o nishphoḷo hue.

22. THE FOX AND THE ADJUTANT BIRD.

English.

Although the fox was not very much given to joking, and was rather given to getting angry, yet one day he came to the determination to make fun of his neighbour the adjutant-bird. After making a great fuss therefore, he invited him to dinner at noon. Meanwhile he had placed different kinds of messes in large but shallow plates. The adjutant-bird afterwards presented itself at the dinner table, but being only able to dip in the point of its beak, in spite of repeated endeavours, it was unable to appease its hunger. In the meanwhile the fox was lapping up, and eating away rapidly, and in pressing his guest to eat he would say: "How do you like all these viands of mine?" The fox was however joking, and the adjutant-bird knowing this, replied, without paying attention to what he said: "Your viands are all of them exceedingly good." Subsequently when taking leave, the adjutant-bird invited the fox so pressingly to come to his house, that the latter found himself quite unable to decline.

Accordingly on the appointed day after the fox had gone to the adjutant-bird's house as he had promised, no sooner were the eatables brought in, than the fox perceived his own great shame, for the adjutant-bird had divided the meat into small pieces, and had quite filled a narrow long-necked vessel with them. The fox not being able to help himself to any of the eatables remained quite hungry, but the adjutant-bird

,,. KO'KI'S'IYA'ḶI' A'U HA'ḌOGIḶA'.

O'ḌIYA'.

Kókís'iyáḷí jodyopi koutukore odhiko roto .no hói práyo tshoḷo koribáre roto tháe tothápi dine góṭáe kókí ihá druḍho monostho kolá: ámbhe áponá poḍósi háḍogiḷá songe poriháṣo koribuñ. Otoebo boḍo áḍomboro kori táháku modhyáhno bhódzono nimonte nimontroṇo kolá. Bádo se nána prokáro dzhóḷo tsounḍá cheptá tháḷire rokhilá. Tohiñre háḍogiḷá bhóḍzono sthánore uposthito hói kéboḷo thonṭoro ogrobhágo dzhóḷore ḍubái párilá, mátro onéko jotno koleheñ khyudhá nibrutto kori párilá náhiñ. Ethimodhyore kókí otis'ighro tsáṭi kháu thaé, puṇi: Kháo ná, kháo ná, éhi kothá bóli áponá nimontrito háḍogiḷáku potsárilá: A'mbho éhi sobu bhokhyo-drobyo tumbhoku kipori láge? Mátro kókís'iyáḷí kéboḷo upohásyo koruochchi, háḍogiḷá ihá dzáṇi táhá kothárе kichchi monojógo no kori kohilá: Tumbho sobu khádyosámogrí oti bholo lágu ochchi. Todbádo bidáyo hebá beḷe háḍogiḷá kókís'iyáḷíku áponá ghoroku jibá nimonte eprokáro druḍhorúpe nimontroṇo kolá je, se kouṇosi prokáre oswíkáro kori párilá náhiñ.

Todbádo sei niyomito dino kókís'iyáḷí áponá botsono onusáre háḍogiḷá ghoroku golá uttáre, jetebeḷe khádyo drobyo uposthito helá tetebeḷe se áponáro boḍo opománo dekhilá; károno, háḍogiḷá guḍáe mángso ṭiki ṭiki kori soru ó lombo goḷá ghoṭore púrṇo kori rokhi tháe. Sei sobu khádyo sámogríro swádo kokís'iyáḷíro grohoṇo koribáku sádhyo no tháe, tohiñre

dipped his long bill into the vessel and filled his stomach full. Afterwards the fox ate up with great gusto any of the food that happened to fall on the outside of the vessel. The adjutant-bird perceiving this then turned towards him, and laughing slightly, said: "I am very glad to see that your appetite is so good." I should like you to eat with as much pleasure as I did on the day of your invitation." The fox upon hearing this speech, lowered his head, and was much displeased. The adjutant-bird thereupon exclaimed: "Do not be annoyed at this affair, for those who are unable to stand a joke themselves, should not attempt jokes upon others."

The moral of this is, that when we attempt a joke upon another man, we should first reflect whether when he returns it, we are able to bear it ourselves or not.

---

23. THE BOYS AND THE FROGS.

A number of frogs were sitting in a large paddy field. At the edge of this field some children began to play roughly with broken pieces of tile, and every now and then showered the pieces into the water. The frogs thereupon became nervous and frightened, and suffered a good deal of anxiety. At last one of the frogs, bolder than the rest, raised his head from the

se kéboḷo bubukhyu hói rohilá. Mátro háḍogiḷá ápoṇá lombá thoṇṭo ghoṭo modhyore déi udoro poripúrṇo kolá. Onontoro kókí ḍonkí uporo piṭhire je kichchi dzhóḷo poḍe táháku boḍo itstshápúrboko tsáṭi kháe. Tetebeḷe háḍogiḷá táhá áḍoku phéri onái olpo hosi kori kohilá, bujhi: Tumbho khyudhá bís'ésho ochchi, é héturu ámbhe boḍo sontushṭo otshuñ. A'mbhe jemonto sehi dino tumbho nimontroṇore khái thiluñ tumbhe modhyo sehirúpe prosonno hói kháo, ehi ámbhoro itstshá.

Kókís'iyáḷí ehi kothá s'uṇi mothá nuáiñ boḍo osontushṭo helá. Tohiñre háḍogiḷá kohilá: "Ehi bishoyore birokto no huo; kipáñki jeuñmáne poriháso sohi no páronti semánongkoro káhári songe poriháso koribáro uchito nuhe."

Iháro tátporjyo éhi, káhári songe koutuko koribáku gole se phéri thoṭṭá kole táhá ámbhemáne sohi páribuñ ki náhiñ é kothá púrbore bitsáro koribá uchito.

---

୬୮. BA'LOKO O' BENGO.

Eko bruhot bilore onéko bengoro bosoti tháe. Táhá dhárore kete guḍáe pilá hoṭhát khoporá kheḷá koribáku lágile, áu páṇire bárombáro khoporá brushṭi kole. Tohiñre bengománe khíṇo ó bhíto hói otis'oyo duḥkho páile. S'éshore somostongkoṭháru sáhási éko bengo biloru mukho boḍhái kohi'á: He priyo báḷoke, tumbhemáne ete s'ighro ápoṇá dzátiro nish-

field, and said : "O dear boys, why do you so early learn the cruel disposition of your race. If you will but reflect, you will find that although this be only play to you, yet it is death to us."

The moral of this is, that it is exceedingly unjust and cruel of us to find any pleasure in the destruction of the comfort and happiness of others.

---

24. THE COWHERD AND THE PEASANTS.

A herdsman who grazed his cattle in a certain plain was frequently in the habit of raising a false alarm and calling out : "Ho! peasants, a tiger has got in amongst my cattle; come to my rescue." Thereupon the peasants hearing the alarm given by the herdsman, would snatch up their sticks and other weapons and run to kill the tiger; but there was no tiger, and they found that the cowherd had only been mocking them. Thus annoyed by the herdsman's deceitful fun, they had to go back again. Some time afterwards a tiger really got into the cattle-fold. The herdsman thereupon began to shout loudly for the peasants, as before, but they, thinking that the herdsman was probably deceiving them, did not go to assist him, and the tiger, after killing several cattle, finally killed the herdsman himself. As the cowherd was dying, he called out and said : "Alas! alas! why did I ever deceive the peasants; when

ṭhuro swobhábo káhiñki s'ikho? bibétsoná kori dekho ehi tumbhománongko kheḷá sotyo, mátro ámbhománongko mrutyu oṭe.

Iháro tátporjyo ehi: Onyoro kus'oḷo ó sukho biná-s'ore ámbhománongkoro áhládo koribáro oti onyáyo ó nishṭhuro oṭe.

---

১৪. GO'ROKHYOKO A'U KRUSHOKO LO'KO.

Kounosi poḍiá modhyore dzoṇe rokhuáḷo góru tsoráu tsoráu bárombáro porihásore mithyá chitkáro s'obdo kori kohe: "He tsosámáne ámbho góru modhy-ore góṭáe byághro ási-ochchi, tumbhemáne ási rokhyá koro." Tohiñre tsosá lóke rokhuáḷoro ehi s'obdo s'uṇi báḍi ó áu áu ostro gheni byághro máribáku jánti, mátro bágho náhiñ, rokhuáḷo protároṇá koru ochchi, ihá dekhonti. E' rúpe rokhúaḷoro mithyá porihásore krushoko lóko birokto hói phéri jánti. Tohiñ uttá-ru dine sotyo góṭáe byághro górupolo modhyoku ásilá. Ethire rokhuáḷo púrbo pori utstsoiswore tsosá lo'kongku ḍákibáku lágiḷá, mátro semáne bibetsoná kole, rokhuáḷo ámbhománongku probontsoná koru-thibo, é héturu kehi rokhyá koribá nimonte táhá nikoṭoku no jibáru byághro onéko góru noshṭo kori s'éshore rokhuáḷoku modhyo bodho kolá. Rokhuáḷo moribá somoyore khedo kori kohibáku lágilá: "Háyo! háyo! púrbore tsosá lókongko songe káhiñ páiñ pro-

ever I shouted for them deceitfully they came, but now that the tiger is killing me, not a man has come to help me."

The moral of this is, that liars are not believed even when they speak the truth.

---

25. THE PADDY-BIRD AND THE SANDPIPER.

A paddy-bird and a sand-piper lived near a certain tank, and fed upon the fish and worms in the paddy-fields. Afterwards it happened not to rain, and the water in the tank drying up, nothing but the mud remained.

The paddy-bird being accustomed to feed on the fish that it caught in the water, and not being in the habit of walking about only in mud, was greatly distressed for want of food, and began to resemble death itself. The sand-piper, however, was able to procure worms from the mud, and as it had plenty to eat, it danced about daily in perfect happiness. The paddy-bird not seeing any other resource, said to the sand-piper very deceitfully: "You lucky fellow, you and I have lived together for a long time in this place, and we both of us drive the same trade, but neither love, friendship nor sympathy exists between us. This is not proper and I am therefore anxious to be upon more intimate terms with you." The sand-piper there-

taroṇá koruthiluñ ; jetebeḷe mithyá tsholore krushokománongku ḍákithiluñ tetebeḷe semáne ásuthile, mátro etebeḷe byághro ámbhoku bodho kolá tothápi kehi ási rokhyá kolá náhiñ."

Iháro tátporjyo éhi : mithyábádi lóko ketebeḷe sotyo kothá kohileheñ kehi bis'wáso kore náhiñ.

---

୬୪. BOKO A'U KA'DUOKHUMPI POKHI'.

Kouṇosi dzoḷás'oyo somípore boko áu káduokhumpi pokhí e duheñ báso koronti ebong ubhoyeṇ biloro motsyo áu kíṭo khánti. Tohiñ uttáru doibát borshe brushṭi nóhibá heturu se dzoḷás'oyo páṇi jáko s'ushko hói kordomo mátro rohilá. Páṇiru motsyo dhori áháro koribáro bokoro obhyáso, otoebo kéboḷo káduore jái no páribáru áháro koshṭore otyonto klés'o pái se mruto práye helá ; mátro káduokhumpiro ponkoru jiá dhori áṇibáro s'oktí thibáru se jotheshṭo áháro khái poromo sukhore protidino nrutyo kore. Boko oti kopoṭí áu onyo upáyo no dekhi káduokhumpi pokhiku kohilá : "A'he bhágyobán tumbhe ámbhe dui dzoṇo bohukáḷo obodhi éhi sthánore báso kori otshuñ, áu eko byobosáyo modhyo koruñ, mátro porosporo ámbho duhingko modhyore áḷápo ki byoboháro ki bhábo náhiñ, eto onuchito ; otoebo tumbho songe bondhutá koribá nimonte ámbhoro itstshá ochchi." Ethire káduokhumpi pokhí bokoro kopoṭo bhábo no dzáṇi swíkáro kolá, puṇi semáne porosporo bondhutá nirúpoṇo

ENGLISH.

upon, not knowing the paddy-bird's deceitful character, gave its consent, and they both of them struck up a mutual friendship. Some days afterwards, the paddy-bird said: "Ah, my friend, the water in the fields has all dried up, and I can catch no fish and am put to much distress for want of food. If you will therefore now give me a little food, I shall be relieved and must remain indebted to you. Besides, if you are ever in distress, I can then repay your kindness. You are moreover now in a position to do a good action, and it is always our duty to render a kindness to others, for there is no greater virtue than to do good to others. Moreover it is the proper thing never to fail to do a kindness to helpless people, for it is of no use providing healthy people with medicine. It is quite certain however that there is some benefit in supplying the sick with it. As I am at present suffering for want of food, give me some therefore and remove my distress." The sand-piper being very compassionate did not suspect anything in the plausible but deceitful proposal of the paddy-bird and taking it under its protection, began to supply it with food. Some days afterwards, there was a great fall of rain, and the paddy-fields being full of water, the paddy-bird exerted itself to catch fish for food. The sand-piper not being able to obtain its food on account of excess of water, now imagined that the paddy-bird, to whom it had done a kindness, would certainly return it. The paddy-bird, however, had no intention of returning its kindness, and was

kole. Kichchi dino uttáre boko kohilá: A'he bondhó bilo páṇi s'ukhi jibáru mátsho dhori no pári, ámbhe onáhárore oti klés'o páu otshuñ é nimonte jebe tumbhe etebeḷe kinchit áháro debo, tebe rokhyá páibuñ áu tumbho sebáre thibuñ; puṇi tumbho bipodokáḷore ámbhe upokáro koribuñ; mátro borttománo upokáro koribá nimonte tumbhoro s'okti ochhi, sorbodá poro upokáro koribáro ámbhománongko korttobyo oṭe, hétu ki poro upokároṭháru odhiko puṇyo áu náhiñ; ebong kátoro lókoro upokáro obos'yo koribáro uchito, káhiñki ná orógi lókoro oushodhodwárá upokáro koribáro nirorthoko, mátro rógi lókoro upokárore lábho ochchi, é kothá promáṇo. E nimonte borttománo ámbhe áháro lági klés'o páu otshuñ túmbhe áháro dei kles'o dúro koro. Káduokhumpi oti doyás'íḷo hói bokoro éhi prokáro kopoṭo soroḷo byoboháror dósho no dhori bokoku ás'rito dzáṇi táku protipáḷono koribáku lágilá. Kichchi dino uttáre mohábrushṭi hebáru bilo poripúrṇo helá, tohiñre boko páṇiru motsyo dhori kháibáro udjógo kolá; áu káduokhumpi odhiko páṇi lági kichchi no pái mone mone kohilá jeuñ bokoro upokáro korithiluñ se obos'yo ámbho upokáro koribo, mátro bokoro protyupokáro koribá dúre tháu, borong se sorbodá káduokhumpiro dósho onusondháno koribáku lágilá, áu onyo kouṇosi dósho no pái kohilá: A're káduokhumpi tumbho onorthoko nrutyo ámbhe sohi no páruñ, é nimonte tumbho lági e stháno tyágo koru otshuñ. Ihá kohi se onyo biloku uḍi golá, áu káduokhumpi onáháro héturu mori golá.

always on the look out to discover some fault in the sand-piper. Not being able however to discover any other fault, it said : "Look here, sand-piper, I really cannot stand your nonsensical dancing about, and I must therefore leave this place on account of you." So saying it flew away to some other field, and the sand-piper died of hunger.

The moral of this is, that deceitful and wicked people make friends, when they themselves are in danger, by divers honeyed words and by plausible but treacherous behaviour, for the sole purpose of obtaining their own ends. Afterwards when they have got what they want, they have no idea of returning the kindness but invent some false excuse to abandon you.

---

26. THE DOG AND THE BULL.

A dog was sleeping upon a heap of grass when a hungry bull came up to eat it, but the dog seeing the bull, loudly growled, and drove it off. Thereupon the bull not venturing to eat the grass for fear of the dog, said to it : "You spiteful creature, you cannot eat this grass yourself, and you will not allow any one else to do so. Very well, this spite will be your ruin." Saying this the bull went away. Afterwards the dog still continuing to guard the grass, died of hunger.

O'ḌIYA'.

Iháro tátporjyo ehi : s'oṭho áu dushṭo lóko ápoṇá ápodo somoyore onyo lóko nikoṭore náná prokáro prítidzonoko bákyo dwárá áu kolpito soroḷo byobohár dwárá keboḷo ápoṇá kárjyo sophoḷo koribá nimonte bhábo kore, tohiñ uttáre kárjyo siddho hele, protyupokáro dúre tháu mithyá kouṇosi dósho dei tyágo koribo.

---

১৯. KUKURO A'U SHOṆḌHO.

Góṭáe kukuro ghásogodá upore s'ói tháe, tohiñre góṭáe shoṇḍho khyudhito hói se gháso kháibá nimonte oilá mátro kukuro shoṇḍhoku dekhi otis'oyo tordzonogordzono kori táku toḍi delá. Ethire shoṇḍho kukuro bhoyo héturu gháso khái no pári kohilá : A're hingsroko, tumbhe é ghásoku ápe kháibo náhiñ áu onyo lókoku khuái debo náhiñ ; bholo é hingsá lági tumbhe nás'o hebo ; ihá kohi shoṇḍho tsáli golá. Todbádo se kukuro gháso rokhyá koru koru onáhárí rohi mori-golá.

ENGLISH.

The moral of this is, that hatred, spite and anger are like fire. Whenever they are found united in any man, they destroy him first. It is a man's duty therefore carefully to guard against all three.

---

27. THE PEASANT AND THE BLACK SNAKE.

As a peasant was walking along the bank of a river very early in the morning in the cold season, he saw a snake nearly dead with cold half buried in the mud. Taking pity upon it, he brought the snake home with much trouble, and after placing it near the fire, he resuscitated it, and protected it by giving it daily milk, plantains, et cetera. The peasant had a son, and the latter from constantly living with the snake became very familiar with it. In this way the snake lived for some time in the peasant's house. One day the peasant's son struck the snake for some reason and no sooner had the snake in obedience to its instincts bitten him than he died. Afterwards the peasant arrived, and seeing that the snake had killed his son by its bite he reproached it severely, and said, "You wicked creature, I saved you when at

O'DIYA'.

Iháro tátporjyo éhi: Dwesho, hingsá, kródho emáne og-ni práye; otoebo ehi sobu johiñru dzáto huonti táháku prothome noshṭo koronti, éhi héturu éhi tiniṭháru sábodháno hói rohibáku monushyongkoro korttobyo ote.

୧୨. TSOSA' A'U KRUSHNOBORṆO SORPO.

Dzoṇe tsosá s'ito ruture oti probhátore kouṇosi nodí tíro dei jáuñ jáuñ kákoro áu ponkore ábruto góṭáe sorpoku mruto práyo dekhilá, áu sọdoyo hói oti jotnore séhi sorpoku ghoroku áṇi og-niro ushṇótá dekhái bontsáilá puṇi proti dino dudho kodoḷí ityádi áháro dei protipáḷono koribáku lágilá. Se tsosáro góṭie putro thilá, táháro sei sọrpo songe sorbodá ekotro báso koribá héturu oti pronoyo helá. Sorpo éhi prokáre tsosá ghore keteko káḷokhyepoṇo kolá bádo, dinoke kouṇosi káronore krushoko putro doṇḍághato kolá, tohiñre sorpo áponá dzátiro dhormánusáre táháku dongs'iba mátroke se práṇo tyágo kolá. Onontore sorpo dongs'onore putro mári-ochchi krushoko ási jetebeḷe ihá dekhilá, tetebeḷe sorpoku onéko bhortsoná kori kohilá: A're pápishṭho tumbhoku mrutyu obostháru bontsái protipáḷono koriluñ taháro ki éhi

the point of death and took care of you, and is this the result?" Hearing this, the snake replied: "I have acted according to the instincts of my nature. You did wrong to treat me with kindness, for ingratitude is the consequence of your mistake."

The moral of this is, that if you do a kindness to spiteful people, ingratitude will be the result.

---

28. THE BELL-METAL MERCHANT.

Two thieves went to a bell-metal seller's shop to buy a vessel, and seeing that the bazar-man was busy with other customers, one of the thieves stole a brass pot, and gave it to his fellow thief who concealed it in the cloth which he wore. Afterwards when the other customers had left, the bell-metal merchant perceived that a brass pot was missing, and immediately seized upon the aforesaid two persons as the thieves. The two thieves, however, denied the fact upon oath. The man who had stolen it, said: "I have not got the brass pot," whilst the man who had hidden it said: "I never took it." Thereupon the bell-metal merchant not being certain as to the thief said: "Good, you have denied the theft, but one of you has most certainly committed theft; be it so, but you will not be able to conceal it from God in whose name you have sworn; for He who is all-wise and the Searcher of hearts knows it, and will award meet punishment for the deed.

pholo ? Iha s'uṇi sorpo kohilá : A'mbho dzátíyo dhormo rokhyá kori-otshuñ ; ámbho upokáro kori tumbhe onuchito kolo, enimonte tumbho nidzo dóshore tumbho opokáro hói-ochchi.

Iháro tátporjyo éhi : Hingsroko lókoro upokáro kole opokáro hue.

---

୬୮. KONGSA' BOṆIKO A'U DUI TSO'RO.

Dui tsóro dzoṇe kongsárí dókánoku básono kroyo koribá nimonte jái dekhile je kongsárí onyányo kretámánongko songe byosto ochhi. Ethimodhyore dzoṇe tsóro góṭie lóṭá tsórí kori ápoṇá songi tsóro hátore delá ; se ápoṇa pindhilá bostro modhyore lutsái rokhilá. Tohiñ uttáre onyo gráhokománe golá bádo kongsárí dekhilá ki góṭie lóṭá náhiñ. Totkhyoṇát se ukto dui dzoṇongku tsóro bóli dhorilá. Tohiñre sedui tsóro s'opotho kori oswíkáro kole jé tsóri kori tháe, se kohilá : Lóṭá ámbhoṭháre náhiñ, áu je lutsái rokhi tháe se kohilá : A'mbheto nei náhuñ. Ethire kongsárí tsóroku nirdrishṭo kori no pári kohilá : Bholo tumbhemáne tsórí oswíkáro kolo mátro tumbhe duhingko modhyoru obos'yo dzoṇe tsórí kori ochchi ; je heu, ámbhoṭháru lutsái otsho, mátro jeuñ Poromes'worongko námore s'opotho kolo táhángkoṭháre ketebeḷe lutsái páribo náhiñ ; kipáñki se sorbognio áu ontoḥrjámí ihá dzáṇonti, ebong é kotháro uchito s'ásti debe.

English.

The moral of this is, that he who commits theft or any other grievous sin is almost certain to be caught, and although he escape detection by man, he will certainly not escape detection by God. He will at least mete out the punishment for it for He is all knowing and all-wise. It is therefore not right for a man to steal.

---

29. THE HUNTER AND THE JACKAL.

A hunter went to a certain forest to hunt, and killed a large boar and a stag. As these two animals were very heavy, the day came to an end as he was carrying them along. The hunter however out of covetousness not liking to abandon the boar and the stag, remained under a mango tree. A black snake was living at the spot and was in the habit of feeding upon such of the mangoes of the tree as were ripe. When the snake saw the hunter, it imagined that he would carry off all the mangoes as soon as day broke, and that in this case, it would be difficult to obtain any for food. It resolved therefore to practise some stratagem in order to prevent the hunter carrying off the mangoes. Having thus determined it bit him. Afterwards the hunter became ill with the strength of the poison and in his anger letting fly an arrow at once killed the snake, and then died himself. A jackal who was near the tree when the hunter arrived had been reflecting that as soon as it became dark, the hunter

O'DIYA'.

Iháro tátporjyo éhi : Tsórí áu máhápátoko kole práyo dhorá poḍe, jodyopi monushyoṭháru uttírṇo hue tothápi Poromes'woronkoṭháru kodátso uttírṇo hebo náhiñ, se táháro protipholo obos'yo debe, károṇo ki se sorbobyápí áu sorbognio oṭonti, otoebo tsóri koribáro monushyongkoro ketebeḷe uchito nuhe.

,,. BYA'DHO A'U S'RUGA'LO.

Dzoṇe byádho kouṇosi bonoku mrugoyá nimonte jái góṭáe boḍo s'úkoro áu góṭáe mrugo márilá. Se dui dzontu oti bhárí hebá héturu gheni ásu ásu dine obosáno helá ; byádho lóbho héturu s'úkoro ó mrugoku tyágo kori jái no pári eko ámbo brukhyo toḷe rohilá. Seṭháre góṭáe káḷosorpo tháe áu brukhyore jete ámbo poripokwo hue táhá sobu kháe, mátro byádhoku dekhi sorpo bibetsoná kolá, e byokti prátoḥ káḷo hebámátroke é ámbo sobu gheni jibo, tohiñre ámbo áháro koshṭo hebo, otoebo johiñre ámbo gheni jái no páribo eprokáro kouṇosi upáyo koribáro uchito. Ihá bhábi táku se dongs'ono kolá. Tohiñ uttáre báṇuá bisho dzwaḷáre pídito hói kródhore báṇo tsháḍi sorpoku totkhyoṇát mári pokáilá ebong ápesuddhá práṇo tyágo kolá. Goṭáe s'rugáḷo sehi brukhyo nikoṭore tháe, áu seṭháku byádho ásibáre se mone mone bibetsoná koruthilá ki rátri hele eṭháro byádho mángso rondhono kori kháibo tohiñru ámbhoku modhyo obós'yo kichchi debo ; kimbá jebe sobu mángso áháro koribo

would cook some meat and eat it, and that he would certainly get some of it, for although the hunter might eat up the meat, yet he would certainly throw away the bones, &c. which the jackal would obtain. But when the jackal saw that the hunter had died from the bite of the snake, and the snake had died by the hunter's arrow, it went under the tree and having obtained so much meat for food without any trouble, it began to reflect that the man would easily last as food for a month, the deer and the boar would last for two months, and the snake would serve as nice food for a day, but for the night it would have to make shift somehow or other, and begin to eat on gradually from the morrow. After reflecting thus, the jackal perceived the hunter's bow, and thought that if it ate the leather bow-string, it would last it for the night. So thinking, it gnawed the string in two, but had no sooner done so, than the bamboo bow rebounded and striking the jackal in the throat, killed it.

The moral of this is, that almost every danger that happens to a man arises from greed. Moreover, if a man accumulates too much, it is a great nuisance. Covetousness and excessive forethought therefore are improper.

30. THE DOVE AND THE BEE.

A bee being very thirsty went to drink in a river and falling into the water, was borne along by

totthápi osthi ityádi pokái debo táhá páibuñ. Todbádo sorpo dongs'ono koribáre báṇúá molá áu báṇúá báṇore sorpo molá, ihá dekhi totkhyoṇát s'rugáḷo brukhyo toḷe pohunchilá : puṇi jothéshṭo khádyo mángso onáyásore pái oti hrushṭo chittore bibetsoná koribáku lágilá, éhi monushyoku porjyonte swotstshondore kháibuñ, mrugo áu boráho é dui ámbhoro dui máso áháro nimonte oṇṭibe, áu sorpo dinoko nimonte bilokhyoṇo bhódzono hebo ; mátro áji rátri kouṇosi prokáre káḷokhyepo kori káliṭháru olpo olpo kháibuñ. Ehi bhábona kori s'rugáḷo byádhoro dhonuko dekhi bibetsono kolá, é dhonuro tsormonirmito guṇo kháile áji rátri jibo ; ihá bhábi dántore sei dhonuro guṇo spors'o kolá mátroke, táhá chhiḍi dhonu báungs'o táhá goḷáre lágibáru s'rugáḷo práṇo tyágo kolá.

Iháro tátporjyo éhi : Monushyoro práyo sobu ápodo lóbhoru dzonme. Punorbáro oti sontsoyo kole oti byágháto hue, énimonte lóbho ó oti sontsoyo okorttobyo.

GHUGHU A'U MOHUMA'CHHI.

Góṭáe mohumácchi trusháre otís'oyo ártto hói nodíre dzoḷo páno koribáku jibáru dzoḷo modhyore poḍi

the current. Meantime a dove seeing the bee's danger bent down the branch of a tree which was on the bank of the river, and the bee clinging to it saved its life. Some days afterwards, the dove was caught in a hunter's net, and the bee seeing by chance that the dove which had saved its own life was in danger, immediately stung the fowler to save it. The fowler thereupon from excessive pain let go the rope of the net, and the dove was saved.

The moral of this is, that if we help others we treasure up good for ourselves. In this world all may help or hinder one another ; it is therefore the duty of all men, both small and great, to assist one another according to their ability

nodí srótore bhási golá. Ethimodhyore góṭáe ghughu pokhi mohumáchhiki bipodogrosto dekhi nodí kúḷore thibá éko brukhyoro ḍálo nodíre nuáiñ delá, sei dáḷo oboḷombono kori mohumáchhi práṇo rokhyá páilá. Kichhi dino uttáre ghughu byádho dzálore poḍilá, áu byádho se dzálo douḍi ṭáṇibáku árombho kolá emonto somoyore mohumáchhi dekhilá, ki nidzo rokhyákorthá ghughu bipodore poḍi-ochhi. Otoebo ghughuro rokhyá nimonte totkhyoṇát byádhoku náhuḍo márilá, tohiñre byádho oti píḍá pái dzálo douḍi tsháḍi debáru ghughu rokhyá páilá.

Iháro tátpórjyo ehi : poro upokáro kole ápoṇá mongoḷoro upáyo sonchito hue. Pruthibí upore somoste porospori upokáro ki opokáro kori páronti ; ehi nimonte tshóṭo boḍo somostongko uchito rúpe upokáro koribáku monushyongkoro korttobyo oṭe.

OFFICIAL TERMS.
KOCHE'RI SOMBONDHO BISHOYO.

English.	O'ḍiyá'.
Abduction, ...	Hori nebáro.
Abetment, ...	Kumoko koribáro.
Abortion, ...	Gorbho nás'o koribáro.
Accomplice, ...	Bháguáḷi.
Acquittal, ...	Ts-háḍi debáro.
Adopted son, ...	Póshiá puo.
Arrest, ...	Dhoribáro.
Arson, ...	Ghore niá logái-debáro.
Auction, ...	Nilámo.
Assault, ...	Piṭibáro.
Bill of Sale, ...	Kroyopotro.
Cheating, ...	Dogá.
Concealing stolen property, ...	Tsóri málo rokhibáro.
Contempt of Court,...	Korṭ ágore durṇoyo.
Criminal Breach of Trust, ...	Bishbásoghátoko dósho koribáro.
Criminal Trespass,...	Dóshojukto probésho.
Criminal Misappropriation, ...	Drobyoku durbyoyo koribáro.
Counterfeit Coin, ...	Roso ṭonká (lit. tin).
Extortion, ...	Boḷotkáre nebáro.
Dacoity, ...	Horiboliyá.

ENGLISH.	O'ḌIYA'.
Gallows, ...	Phásikhombo.
Guilty, ...	Dóshi.
Handcuffs, ...	Hátohoḍi.
Heir, ...	Hokodáro.
House-breaking,......	Sindho Tsóri.
Hurt, ...	Upodrobo.
False evidence, ...	Mits-ho sákhyo.
Infanticide,...........	Báḷoko hotyá.
Intimidate, ...	Ḍoráibáro.
Mad, ...	Báyá.
Murder, ...	Khuṇí.
Mischief,..............	Nás'o.
Oath, ...	Niámo.
Offence, ...	Dósho.
Paper, ...	Kágodzo.
Pregnant, ...	Gorbho.
Rape, ...	Boḷotkáre romoṇo koribáro.
Robbery,..............	Ghátojukto tsóri.
Rebellion, ...	Méḷi.
Sand, ...	Báli.
Seal, ...	Mudrá.
Signature, ...	Sontoko.
Simple Theft,........	Sádhárono Tsóri.
Suicide, ...	A'tmághàto dósho.
Unlawful Assembly,..	Okromore pundzá koribáro.

NUMERALS. ONKOMA'NE.

1	Eko.	31	Ekotiris'i.
2	Dui.	32	Bottis'i.
3	Tini.	33	Tettis'i.
4	Tsári.	34	Tsoutiris'i.
5	Pántso.	35	Pontsotiris'i.
6	Ts-ho.	36	Ts-hotis'i.
7	Sáto.	37	Sototiris'i.
8	A'ṭho.	38	Oṭhotiris'i.
9	No.	39	Oṇotsális'i.
10	Doso.	40	Tsális'i.
11	Egáro.	41	Ekotsális'i.
12	Báro.	42	Boyális'i.
13	Téro.	43	Téyális'i.
14	Tsoudo.	44	Tsourális'i.
15	Pondoro.	45	Pointsális'i.
16	Shóholo.	46	Ts-hotsális'i.
17	Sotoro.	47	Sototsális'i.
18	Oṭhoro.	48	Oṭhotsális'i.
19	Oṇáis'i.	49	Oṇotsáso.
20	Kóḍie.	50	Potsás'o.
21	Ekois'i.	51	Ekábono.
22	Báis'i.	52	Bááno.
23	Téis'i.	53	Tepono.
24	Tsobis'i.	54	Tsoubono.
25	Ponchis'i.	55	Pontsábono.
26	Ts-hobis'i.	56	Ts-hopono.
27	Sotáis'i.	57	Sotábono.
28	Oṭháis'i.	58	Oṭhábono.
29	Oṇotiris'i.	59	Oṇosháṭhi.
30	Tiris'i.	60	Sháṭhie.

61	᱆᱁	Ekoshoṭhi.	81	᱈᱁	Ekás í.
62	᱆᱂	Báshoṭhi.	82	᱈᱂	Boyás í.
63	᱆᱃	Téshoṭhi.	83	᱈᱃	Téyás í.
64	᱆᱄	Tsoushoṭhi.	84	᱈᱄	Tsourás'í.
65	᱆᱅	Pontsoshoṭhi.	85	᱈᱅	Pontsás í.
66	᱆᱆	Ts-hoshoṭhi.	86	᱈᱆	Ts-hoyás 'í.
67	᱆᱇	Sotoshoṭhi.	87	᱈᱇	Sotás'í.
68	᱆᱈	Oṭhoshoṭhi	88	᱈᱈	Oṭhás'í.
69	᱆᱉	Oṇosturi.	89	᱈᱉	Oṇonou.
70	᱇᱀	Sotturi.	90	᱉᱀	Noue.
71	᱇᱁	Ekosturi.	91	᱉᱁	Ekáṇói.
72	᱇᱂	Básturi.	92	᱉᱂	Boyáṇói.
73	᱇᱃	Tésturi.	93	᱉᱃	Téyáṇói.
74	᱇᱄	Tsousturi.	94	᱉᱄	Tsouráṇói.
75	᱇᱅	Pontsosturi.	95	᱉᱅	Pontsáṇọi.
76	᱇᱆	Ts-hosturi.	96	᱉᱆	Ts-hoyáṇói.
77	᱇᱇	Sotosturi.	97	᱉᱇	Sotáṇói.
78	᱇᱈	Oṭhosturi.	98	᱉᱈	Oṭháṇói.
79	᱇᱉	Oṇás'i.	99	᱉᱉	Onés'woto.
80	᱈᱀	Os'ie.	100	᱁᱀᱀	S'oye, or S'o

1000	᱁᱀᱀᱀	Hodzáro.
10000	᱁᱀᱀᱀᱀	Oyuto.
100000	᱁᱀᱀᱀᱀᱀	Lokhyo.
1000000	᱁᱀᱀᱀᱀᱀᱀	Niyuto.
10000000	᱁᱀᱀᱀᱀᱀᱀᱀	Kóṭie.